grammar

Ron Simpson

Hodder Education
338 Euston Road, London NW1 3BH.

Hodder Education is an Hachette UK company

First published in UK 2011 by Hodder Education.

British Library Cataloguing in Publication Data: a catalogue record for this title
is available from the British Library.

10 9 8 7 6 5 4 3 2 1

The publisher has used its best endeavours to ensure that any website
addresses referred to in this book are correct and active at the time of going
to press. However, the publisher and the author have no responsibility for the
websites and can make no guarantee that a site will remain live or that the
content will remain relevant, decent or appropriate.

The publisher has made every effort to mark as such all words which it
believes to be trademarks. The publisher should also like to make it clear that
the presence of a word in the book, whether marked or unmarked, in no way
affects its legal status as a trademark.

Every reasonable effort has been made by the publisher to trace the copyright
holders of material in this book. Any errors or omissions should be notified in
writing to the publisher, who will endeavour to rectify the situation for any
reprints and future editions.

Hachette UK's policy is to use papers that are natural, renewable and
recyclable products and made from wood grown in sustainable forests.
The logging and manufacturing processes are expected to conform to the
environmental regulations of the country of origin.

www.hoddereducation.co.uk

Typeset by MPS Limited, a Macmillan Company.
Printed in Great Britain by CPI Cox & Wyman, Reading.

Contents

1

nouns

Nouns and verbs are the basic building blocks of the English language. In traditional terms the noun is a 'naming word' and the verb 'a word of doing or being'. Hence the simplest of statements (English grammar at its most basic) consists of a name and what he/she/it did: 'Jesus wept.'

An understanding of nouns and verbs is central to our knowledge of English grammar. Not only do they form the material of simple statements, but many other parts of speech (notably pronouns, adjectives and adverbs) can be understood only in relation to nouns and verbs.

This chapter deals with the different types of noun, considering the differences between proper, common and collective nouns. It also explains some of the uses of nouns and the ways nouns form their plurals and touches on some of the different noun equivalents.

Common and proper nouns

The definition 'naming word' has potential for confusing the unwary student. You are familiar with 'name' as something individual, the name of a city, person, club, association or firm. Nouns are more often the name not of an **individual**, but of a **species**, **genre** or **type**. You have a name that applies to yourself individually (*Margaret, Mr Rowley* or whatever), but there are many other nouns that can be applied to you as a type or member of a group. Take your pick from such words as: *student, woman, youth, sportsman, driver, worker, painter, cleaner, campaigner* or *couch-potato*.

A **common noun** is one that applies to the group or type: it is common to all. For example, *singer, town, sword, tea, politician, regiment, actor*.

A **proper noun** is one that applies to the individual. For example, *Callas, Weymouth, Excalibur, Typhoo, Cameron, Grenadier Guards, Olivier*.

All proper nouns begin with a capital letter

A slight exception occurs in the case of names (proper nouns) that consist of more than one word. The tendency in such cases is not to use a capital letter at the start of any 'unimportant' word. So both words in *Daily Mail* have capitals, but not every word in *News of the World*. Or compare the titles of two Graham Greene novels: *Brighton Rock* and *The Power and the Glory*.

Collective nouns

A **collective noun** is the name of a group comprising several (many?) individual parts. It is very straightforward to think of words such as: *class, team, herd, committee, association, collection, staff, fleet, flock, group* (of course) or (in some senses) *party*.

The difficulty is that, strictly speaking, a collective noun is **singular** (i.e. refers to one thing only), but sometimes our instincts are to regard it as **plural** (referring to more than one) because of the many individuals involved. It is natural to say, 'The fleet's in', but it is equally natural to say, 'The class *have* had enough of English grammar.'

Abstract and concrete nouns

Another broad distinction is between abstract and concrete nouns. **Concrete nouns** are described as 'material', **abstract nouns** as 'immaterial'. This means, simply, that concrete nouns exist in a physical form, are there to be seen, touched or tripped over, while abstract nouns have no existence that can be determined by the senses of sight, touch or even smell.

Take the sentence, 'We crossed the meadows in hope, expecting soon to see the beauty of the daffodils.' There are four nouns there, two **concrete** referring to things with a physical form (*meadows, daffodils*), two **abstract** referring to emotions or concepts (*hope, beauty*).

Number: singular and plural

Like so much in English grammar, the question of **number** becomes a problem only in the exceptions to the rule. Modern distinctions between **count nouns** and **mass (non-count) nouns** need not worry the general student of English grammar. Certainly some nouns can form a plural (count nouns) and some cannot (mass nouns). However, many nouns can operate as either. A recent book cited *homework* as an example of a mass noun, unable to form a plural, but how many schoolteachers have said to their students, 'You've missed *three homeworks*!'?

What matters is the correct formation of the **plural**. The majority of nouns form the plural by adding *s*, but there are many exceptions.

Sibilants

To make them easy to say, words ending in a sibilant (*s, z, x, sh, ch*, etc.) add an *e* to make an extra syllable: *mass/masses, quiz/quizzes, fox/foxes, marsh/marshes, church/churches*, etc.

y into *ies*

A rule that is easy to learn and almost without exceptions is to replace *y*, if it follows a consonant at the end of a noun, with *ies* in the plural: *factory/factories, story/stories, country/countries*. Note that this does not apply if the *y* follows a vowel. In particular, be careful with *-ey*: *story* (a tale) becomes *stories, storey* (the floor of a building) becomes *storeys*.

-ves or not

The practice concerning words ending in *f* or *fe* is rather more difficult. Some form the plural by changing the ending to *-ves*; some form the plural in the normal way; in some cases, both versions are correct. Unfortunately it is simply a matter of learning which are which and being sensitive to pronunciation. The way in which we say *knives, loaves, halves, lives*, etc., tells us the spelling. *Chiefs, griefs, proofs* and *gulfs* are similarly straightforward. With *roofs/rooves, hoofs/hooves, scarfs/scarves* and *dwarfs/dwarves* you must decide for yourself where you stand.

o for an ending

Words ending in *o* can also cause confusion. Many like *potatoes* and *tomatoes* add an extra *e*, but many others form the plural in the normal way: *pianos, folios, cameos, solos, cellos, concertos*. Interestingly many of these are of Italian origin and the plurals end in *i* in the original. You will find *celli, concerti*, etc., in English, but usually only in specialist music writing: 'Handel wrote many *concerti* grossi', but 'The *Emperor* is one of my favourite piano *concertos*'.

No change

In some cases nouns have **zero plural**; in other words, they remain unchanged in the plural. These are, most notably, nouns referring to animals, maybe because we often see animals in both number and mass. We may eat/keep as a pet/be attacked by an individual animal, but we also make our living by breeding *cattle* or order *salmon* for a meal. Other cases include *sheep, deer, cod, grouse* and *trout*.

Foreign origins

If a foreign word is taken into the English language without change, there is a tendency to use the original foreign plural (often *a* for *um* words derived from Latin). The soundest advice is:

* When a word is so fully absorbed that we think of it as an English word, it is probably wiser to form the plural with *s*: *stadiums* and *gymnasiums* now seem more natural than *stadia* and *gymnasia*, though the latter two are not wrong.

* When the original plural becomes established in its own right, then use it. The best example is *data*, much more widely used than *datum*. Anyone using *datums* to mean 'given facts' would simply spread confusion.

* There are many cases where personal choice is all that matters. You may use *radii* because *radiuses* sounds cumbersome; *addenda* may continue to be used because it has little currency in ordinary conversation, but *radiuses* and *addendums* are perfectly acceptable words. The plural of *genius* can be *genii* or *geniuses*. Many people use *geniuses* for astonishingly gifted people and *genii* for spirits. In the same way the context can have an effect. For instance, what word do you use for more than one cactus? Usually, looking at them as a mass in a garden centre, we would say, 'That's a fine display of *cacti*.' Singling them out individually and in the tough world of the Hollywood Western, the besieged leader of the wagon train would perceive the Apaches hiding behind the *cactuses*.

en plurals

The *en* ending for plurals is an ancient and once common form. Appropriately enough, apart from *children*, it tends to be used in rather old-fashioned contexts. *Oxen* and *brethren* are two such examples. *Brethren*, of course, means the same as *brothers*, but the situations where it is used are quite different. *Brethren* usually has a biblical or religious context: *Joseph and his Brethren* or *The Plymouth Brethren*.

Change the vowel

Derived from Old English, the plural of several common nouns involves changing the central vowel rather than adding an ending. Many of the irregular and old-fashioned plurals apply to nouns which were staples of existence before the regular *s* ending became common. Just like the zero plural, the **vowel change plural** applies to several animals (*goose/geese, mouse/mice*), plus parts of the body (*tooth/teeth, foot/feet*) and, of course, *man/men* and *woman/women*. A variation on this is the archaic plural of cow (*kine*) which you may still find in old Bible stories.

Compound nouns

Some nouns are made up of two or more words (**compounds**). Which one is turned into the plural? It is impossible to lay down an exact rule, but it is probably best to focus on the main noun in those cases where hyphens are used (*daughters-in-law, lords-lieutenant*; in ranks such as *Major-Generals* the second word is the more important) and to place the *s* at the end where they have become one word (*cupfuls, bucketfuls*).

Nouns in apposition

Nouns in any part of the sentence can be modified by the addition of adjectives, adjective phrases or adjective clauses. However, the information given about a noun can also be enlarged by placing another noun, noun phrase or noun clause **in apposition**. This term is used when two or more nouns or noun equivalents are placed next to each other, each of them referring to the same person or thing so that the sentence would still make sense if one of them was removed. Let us imagine that Mrs Lindley is the Chair of Governors at a school. The secretary could tell the Head:

Mrs Lindley (proper noun) *has arrived*.

or

The Chair of Governors (noun phrase) *has arrived*.

If the two were combined in the sentence

Mrs Lindley, the Chair of Governors, has arrived.

they would be in apposition.

To take another example, here are two ways you could tell the reader more about Charles Dickens' novel *The Mystery of Edwin Drood*:

The Mystery of Edwin Drood, *set in a fictional version of Rochester*, was never finished.
The Mystery of Edwin Drood, *Charles Dickens' final novel*, was never finished.

In the first example the section in italics is an adjectival phrase; in the second it is a noun phrase in apposition. Note that the sentence would make sense if the title of the novel was omitted.

Noun equivalents: noun clauses

Pronouns, noun phrases and noun clauses can all be considered as **noun equivalents**. However, it is important to your study of the noun to remember that noun clauses are often not built around a key noun. A noun clause carries out the same function as a noun. In the sentence 'Why I am leaving is none of your business', the subject is the noun clause, *Why I am leaving*. There is a pronoun in it, but there is no noun that relates to the meaning of the subject: *my reasons*.

We might write:

I found it hard to understand *his methods*.

In this case the direct object is *methods*, but we could replace that with a noun phrase with no equivalent word:

I found it hard to understand *how he did it*.

pronouns

In terms of function, pronouns are the same as nouns. If you write, 'She lives next door to my mother', the word *she* takes the same role in the sentence as *Mrs Robinson* does in, 'Mrs Robinson lives next door to my mother'. *Mrs Robinson* is a proper noun, *she* is a pronoun. In this case the prefix *pro-* means 'in place of', so a pronoun is simply a word that can take the place of a noun. Replacing nouns with pronouns can be simpler and less monotonous, but also (at times) confusing.

The most common type of pronoun is the personal pronoun, the only way of referring to the person(s) speaking or writing and the person(s) being spoken or written to, and often a convenient way of referring to other people or things. However, there are many other types of pronoun the most common of which are explained here.

What makes the following paragraph so boring?

> The policeman examined the document carefully. At first
> the policeman seemed convinced that the document was
> genuine, but then the policeman noticed the alteration to
> the signature. The policeman turned the document over
> and revealed the false serial number. The policeman pushed
> the document toward the prisoner.

Certainly some names, wider vocabulary and rephrasing
would help, but above all the repetition of *policeman* and *document*
is monotonous: the use of *he* and *it* (pronouns) is desperately
needed:

> The policeman examined the document carefully. At first he
> seemed convinced that it was genuine, but then he noticed
> the alteration to the signature, etc.

Personal pronouns

Personal pronouns take the place of personal nouns, though
you must remember that the neuter *it* is also a personal pronoun.
Additionally they form the only way of referring to certain people.
Personal pronouns can relate to two different persons or groups of
persons not normally covered by nouns:

* the person speaking or writing or the people of whom
  he/she is one;
* the person(s) being spoken or written to.

These are known as the **first person** (*I, me, we, us*) and the
second person (*you*). The other pronouns are in the **third person**.
All nouns are customarily thought of as in the **third person**.
Situations where a speaker/writer may refer to him/herself by a
noun are few, sometimes suggesting arrogance: e.g. Shakespeare's
Julius Caesar: 'Shall Caesar send a lie?', 'Caesar doth not wrong',
etc. You might find a journalist referring to him/herself as 'your
correspondent', blurring the distinction between first and third
person, but this is rare.

Case in personal pronouns

English is a language that has virtually done away with **case**. In Latin and many of the languages derived from it, a noun takes a different form if it is used as the subject of a sentence or the object or in a certain type of phrase or showing possession. These different forms are known as **cases**: the **nominative** if the noun is the subject, the **accusative** if it is the object, the **genitive** if indicating possession, etc. Pronouns provide one of the few examples in English of the continuing use of cases. In the following chart the terms nominative and accusative are replaced by the more familiar **subjective** and **objective**:

	Singular	
	Subjective	Objective
1st person	I	me
2nd person	you	you
3rd person masculine	he	him
3rd person feminine	she	her
3rd person neuter	it	it
	Plural	
1st person	we	us
2nd person	you	you
3rd person	they	them

The subjective is used when the pronoun is the subject of the sentence ('*She* went on holiday'). The objective is used when the pronoun is the object of the sentence ('The receptionist called *her* to the phone') or of a preposition ('Her children ran to *her*'). Because the case is identified by the word itself, it means that word order is less important than is usual in English. Though it sounds very old-fashioned, you could write '*Him* smote *I* with my mighty sword' and it would make sense. This is not possible with nouns where the word order indicates who is striking the blow. Just imagine a sentence like, 'Goliath killed David with a stone

from his sling'. The meaning is reversed, but 'Goliath killed *he*
with a stone from his sling' retains the correct meaning, though
it does sound old-fashioned and awkward.

Gender in personal pronouns

One of the problems in the use of personal pronouns can
arise because of the identification of gender. Where the person is
identified, there is no difficulty: *he* or *she* is used. Sometimes, when
the person is not identified, the context removes all (or nearly all)
doubts:

> When the manageress appeared, *she* sorted out the bill.
> The actor said *he* thought that playing Hamlet was the
> greatest challenge of *his* life.

Though there have been female Hamlets, both of the above
are fairly safe, as are all cases in the plural (*they/them*). But what
are you to do with the following sentence?

> When an inexperienced teacher starts work, *** must expect
> to be confronted by a range of problems.

They is ungrammatical (singular turned into plural), though
its use is becoming more accepted. *He* is possibly inaccurate
and probably sexist. *He or she* is accurate and would fit here, but
constant use throughout the following sentences would become
monotonous. *He or she/him or her* have their uses (certainly in
documents, reports, circulars, etc.), but they seldom sound or read
like natural idiomatic English. In the above case you can turn the
whole thing into the plural:

> When inexperienced teachers start work, they must expect
> to be confronted by a range of problems.

Ambiguity in personal pronouns

Care needs to be taken with the use of personal pronouns
when writing about more than one individual of the same gender.

He, *she* and *it* cannot be modified to indicate two or three separate boys or women or garden sheds. The following examples show the possibilities for confusion:

> The Branch Manager told the salesman that he had left early last Thursday.
>
> Mrs Tate told her daughter to ask the teacher if she would mind if she brought the reply slip in to her just before she went to London.

It may be that, in context (the phrases and sentences surrounding them), these examples may become clear. This is purely a matter of judgement, not rules. If you think that the meaning is ambiguous, there are various ways of solving the problem. The most obvious is to replace some of the pronouns with nouns. If you are writing a report where clarity is the only requirement, you might write, 'she (the teacher)', but in ordinary writing you would look to be a little more subtle. Remember that it is always possible to recast the whole sentence:

> Mrs Tate planned to bring in the reply slip just before her daughter went to London. She told Louise to check with her teacher that this was not too late.

Reflexive pronouns

Though personal pronouns are the most frequently used of pronouns, there are several other common types. The most similar in form to personal pronouns are **reflexive pronouns**:

1st person singular	myself
2nd person singular	yourself
3rd person singular	himself/herself/itself
1st person plural	ourselves
2nd person plural	yourselves
3rd person plural	themselves

Reflexive pronouns have two functions. Their main task is to indicate that the action is 'reflected' back on the doer, that the subject has done something to him/herself:

I've hurt myself quite badly.
The Managing Director gave herself a huge pay increase.

However, reflexive pronouns (sometimes referred to as **emphasizing pronouns** in this use) can also emphasize a noun or a personal pronoun. What is the difference between the following sentences?

The Queen is due to visit the factory.
The Queen *herself* is due to visit the factory.

There is no difference at all, except that it is rather impressive that the reigning monarch is coming, so *herself* emphasizes the surprise, delight, awe or even fear that the visit brings. Alternatively the emphasis may be due not to the status or importance of the person, but his/her significance in the story being told or the fact that he/she has been the main focus of interest:

Jane laid on three goals with her clever stick-work before she *herself* scored the fourth.

The use of reflexive pronouns for emphasis is purely a matter of taste and should not be overdone.

Relative pronouns

Relative pronouns establish a relationship between objects or people in different clauses: in other words, the same noun is involved in both clauses. The **relative pronoun** serves to join the clauses into one sentence and combines the functions of *and* and the noun or pronoun in question. For example:

Mrs Brown took her children to school every day. She was worried by the traffic on the main road.

people and you should not find it difficult to understand a textbook whichever definition it employs.

Other forms of pronoun

a The relative pronouns (*what*, *who*, *whom*, *whose* and *which*) can also be used in question (**interrogative**) form:

What did you find in the cupboard?
Who was that lady?

In the example, 'Which book did you choose?', *which* is strictly an interrogative adjective, telling us about the noun *book*.

b There are also two linked groups of pronouns which often cause difficulty because they are always **singular** even though they might refer to more than one person or thing. *Each*, *every*, *either* and *neither*, plus *everyone* and *everything*, can be called **distributive pronouns** because they separate items whereas *all* and *both* (which are **plural**) bring together persons or things. This is easy to see in a sentence like:

Either of them is likely to get the job.

In that case, you know that, though both have a chance, only one will be appointed. The meaning of 'Both of them are likely to get the job' is quite different. In the second case we expect two people (not one) to be employed.

On the other hand, things are rather more complicated in:

Each has passed the examination.

In this case many people (4, 30, 200?) have passed the examination, but the grammatical justification is that the sentence is making the statement about each candidate individually.

c *Any*, *anyone*, *anything*, *someone*, *somebody*, *nothing*, *nobody* and *no one* (two words) can be referred to as indefinite pronouns and also take the singular:

Anyone is capable of understanding the situation.
Somebody has to take responsibility for the loss.

3

verbs

Analysis of the forms and functions of verbs can be extremely complicated. For instance, the various tenses can be given imposing, but confusing, names. Therefore it is important always to remember that verbs essentially are words of doing or being. A verb conveys an action performed or can aid a comment on the state of affairs, emotions, conditions, etc.

This chapter will consider the various types of verb. Verbs can be classified in many different ways: the distinction between transitive and intransitive (taking or not taking an object) is important, but probably the most crucial division is between the finite (or tensed) and non-finite forms of the verb.

Other matters dealt with include the difference between the active and the passive voice, how to form tenses (the forms of verb relating to different times) and the uses of auxiliary verbs (verbs that assist in forming tenses).

Verbs of doing: transitive and intransitive

There are some actions that are complete in themselves: *sleeping, waiting, screaming*. The reader may be interested in where you are sleeping, what you are waiting for or why you are screaming, but such information is not necessary to make sense of the statement:

In a corner of the room the guard was sleeping.

This is a fuller statement than the simple 'The guard was sleeping', but the shorter statement still makes sense in its own right. *Sleep* is an **intransitive verb**.

Other verbs do not make complete sense until you add an object: the 'done to' person or thing. It makes no sense to say that you *poured* or *opened* or *appointed* unless you say who or what you poured, opened or appointed:

Yesterday we appointed a new office manager.

Manager is the object of *appointed*, a **transitive verb**.

Many verbs can be transitive or intransitive, but you should be able to work out which way a verb is being used. For example:

She *runs* in the park every morning. (intransitive)
She is planning to *run* a half-marathon. (transitive – object *half-marathon*)
She even finds time to *run* the guide troop. (transitive – object *guide troop*)

Lie and lay

The transitive/intransitive problem lies behind one of the most common errors in English: the confusion of the verbs *to lie* and *to lay*. It does not help that the past tense of *to lie* is *lay*, the same as the present tense of *to lay*. *To lay* is **transitive**, so it is correct to write or speak about 'laying eggs', 'laying cards on the table', 'laying your hand on someone' or 'laying a ghost'. It is not correct to refer to 'laying down for an hour'. That is **intransitive** and requires the use of *to lie*: 'lying down for an hour'.

Verbs of being

Verbs of the third basic category, **verbs of being**, are much fewer in number. *To be* (with all its strange forms such as *am*, *is*, *was* and *were*) is the main one and the other verbs of being fulfil a similar function. For instance, we might take the sentence:

Mrs Bradshaw was very well informed about the novels of Dickens.

This states what is so. If you wish to state that, as far as you can tell, she is well informed, but you are not sure, you might write:

Mrs Bradshaw seemed (or appeared) well informed about the novels of Dickens.

If she used not to be well informed, but developed her knowledge gradually, you would probably express it as:

Mrs Bradshaw became very well informed about the novels of Dickens.

Clearly *seemed*, *appeared* and *became* are fulfilling the same function as 'was' and are therefore verbs of being.

Verbs of being require something to complete their meaning, just as do transitive verbs. However, following a verb of being, clearly nothing or nobody has suffered the action (there is no action), so these are not objects, but **complements**, also known as **intensive complements**. A complement is something which completes, and the intensive complement completes the meaning of the verb of being.

Nouns and pronouns as intensive complements

One of the most common forms of complement occurs when the complement echoes the subject in the form of a noun:

That man is Mr Patel.

That man (subject) and *Mr Patel* (complement) are equivalents, referring to the same man. Even in more complicated sentence structures, the same form can often be detected:

> The result of the financial state of the new theatre trust is likely to be the resignation of the treasurer and half the committee.

Despite the many phrases and the longer sentence it is possible to pick out the equation: *result* (subject) = *resignation* (complement).

At the other extreme, a sentence as simple as 'This is it' provides another example of the same sentence structure, in this case with pronouns as subject and complement.

Adjectives as intensive complements

If the purpose of the sentence is to describe the subject, rather than just identify him/her, the verb of being can be followed by an adjective or adjectival phrase. The structure is identical to that described above:

> The current MP seems *the best candidate*. (complement noun)
> The current MP seems *very efficient*. (complement adjective)
> The Mansion House is *a fine 18th-century building*.
>   (complement noun)
> The Mansion House is *most impressive*. (complement adjective)

Adverbial complements

The final main form of the intensive complement involves using an adverbial phrase to complete the statement. In these cases the relationship with the subject is still evident, but the complement expresses *When?* or *Where?* rather than *Who?* or *What?*:

> The clock was *on top of the cupboard*.
> Her birthday seemed *too far away*.

The same adverbial phrase can be used simply to modify the verb, but in the cases above it **completes** the meaning of the verb. Compare the two following examples:

> My new pen is *in my pocket*.
> My new pen is *safe* in my pocket.

In the first example *in my pocket* is the complement of the verb *is*. In the second example *safe* is the adjectival complement and *in my pocket* is an adverbial phrase modifying the verb and its complement.

Finite and non-finite verbs

The major distinction in the form of verbs is between the **finite (tensed)** and **non-finite (non-tensed)** forms. A finite verb has a **tense** and takes a subject; this means that a finite form of the verb tells you *when it happened* and *who/what did/was it*. Broadly tenses can be defined as **past, present** and **future**:

Vicky *trains* hard. (present)
Vicky *trained* hard last year. (past)
Vicky *will train* hard once she gets a place in the first team. (future)

We are told the subject of the sentences (*Vicky*) and what time each sentence relates to. *Trains*, *trained* and *will train* are finite verbs.

The main non-finite forms are past and present participles and the infinitive (i.e. the basic form: *to work, to be*, etc.). A non-finite verb does not give information on time and cannot take a subject without the use of an auxiliary verb. *Training* is the present participle, but it does not indicate that the action takes place in the present. The auxiliary verb dictates the tense and allows the use of a subject:

Vicky *training* hard. (present participle: this does not make sense as a sentence, though it could be a caption to a picture)
Vicky *is training* hard. (present participle used with auxiliary (*is*) referring to the present)
Vicky *was training* hard. (present participle with different auxiliary (*was*) now refers to past)

We will examine tenses and participles in more detail, but you need to be clear about the distinction between finite and non-finite verbs: **every full sentence must contain at least one finite verb.**

Tenses can be formed by:

* alterations to the stem of the verb;
* use of an auxiliary (helping) verb: *have*, *will*, *to be*, etc.
  The auxiliary is used with a non-finite part of the verb
  to create the desired tense: infinitive (*will find*), present
  participle (*are finding*), past participle (*have found*).

The two tenses formed by changes to the verb itself are
the **present** and the **simple past** (often referred to as the
preterite).

The present tense

This is very straightforward, often the same as the infinitive,
with -*s* added for the third person singular, with an inevitable extra
e when pronunciation requires it following a sibilant last consonant
or multiple consonants like -*sh*, -*ch* and -*tch*:

The dog barks.   Time passes.   She catches the bus.

Irregular forms are not a problem, though, of course, *to be*
pursues an eccentric course, mainly using *are*, but including *I am*
and *he/she/it is*.

The present tense in English is used:

* to indicate events happening now;
* to refer to events that happen regularly, even if they are
  not occurring at this moment.

For instance, in the middle of the week, you are quite likely
to say:

Jenny *goes* into town on Saturday mornings. I *saw* her in the
   market last week.

Jenny is not going into town at present (it is, after all,
Wednesday, not Saturday); you know she went there in the past
(hence the verb *saw*); you expect her to go there in the future.
However, the present tense is correct as referring to an action that,
as things are, happens regularly.

Continuous tenses

Any tense in English can have its continuous form and, as the **present continuous** is much used, this is a good place to consider them, but these comments apply equally to **past continuous**, **future continuous**, etc. A continuous tense (which uses the present participle) represents, naturally enough, an action that is continuing; in other words, you do not see it end:

Pat *prepares* the final draft. (present)
Pat *is preparing* the final draft now. (present continuous)

The first sentence tells of a decision or a regular practice; the second indicates what is going on now. The present continuous does not indicate a successful (or unsuccessful) outcome. Pat may open the door in a minute's time with the work complete or with an apology that she is having problems with her computer.

Simple past tense (preterite)

What we will define as **weak verbs** and **strong verbs** form their past tenses in different ways. The **weak verb** (which we can also call **regular**) simply adds -*ed* (or -*d* for verbs ending in *e*) to the basic form of the infinitive. In some, very few cases -*t* can replace -*ed* (*burn/burned* or *burnt*). Final consonants are doubled when it is necessary to keep a short vowel sound in the preceding syllable:

help/helped	*talk/talked*
trip/tripped	*fire/fired*
reminisce/reminisced	*pad/padded*

With weak (regular) verbs the past tense and past participle are usually identical.

The **strong verbs** form the past tense by altering the central vowel of the basic form, sometimes making other changes as well: *buy*, for instance, becomes *bought* and *leave* turns into *left*. More often it is simply the vowel sound that changes:

shoot/shot	*strive/strove*
fight/fought	*give/gave*
find/found	*blow/blew*
grow/grew	*bind/bound*

The strongest and most irregular of verbs in forming the past tense are *to be* (inevitably) and *to go*. Each of these assumes a totally different identity in the past tense (*was/were* and *went*) before reverting to a comparatively conventional infinitive + *(e)n* for the past participle: *been/gone*. Be sure to avoid constructions like *He's went* in writing, though in some areas it is common practice in speech.

The fact that the verb *to be*, unlike other verbs, distinguishes between singular and plural in the past tense also needs care. *We was* is quite a common usage and *I* (or *he/she/it*) *were* is normal speech across much of the north of England. However, neither is acceptable in formal speech or written English.

Tenses formed using auxiliary verbs: perfect tenses

The main tenses formed with auxiliary verbs can be split into two pairs:

1 the (**present**) **perfect** and **past perfect**, and
2 the **future** and **future in the past**.

The two perfect tenses use the auxiliary verb *to have* with the past participle and the only real difficulty with the form of the tense concerns the past participle of strong verbs (dealt with above). Its usage is somewhat more complex. The **perfect** or **present perfect** implies an action in the past which may be complete (perfect), but which continues to the present (hence present perfect). For instance, we might take these examples:

Fiona *finished* her lunch. (simple past or preterite)
Fiona *has finished* her lunch. (present perfect)

In each case the action is complete, but the first could refer to any time (it might even refer to a visit Fiona made at lunchtime a week ago) whereas the second implies a recent completion. If we say 'Mrs Ross *has left* the building', we are implying that this is the latest information. If we know she left two hours ago, we would say: 'Mrs Ross *left* the building two hours ago/at 3 o'clock/when she had completed the survey.'

The **past perfect** (sometimes called the **pluperfect**) is in relation to the past as the perfect is to the present; it is one stage further back in time.

Tenses formed using auxiliary verbs: future tenses

The **future tense** as such is formed by adding the auxiliary *will* or *shall* to the basic form of the infinitive (minus *to*). Apart from the distinction between *shall* and *will* (see below) this is very straightforward and refreshingly exception-free:

> Our coach will leave at 5 o'clock. There will be three stops after Doncaster. The coach will arrive in Newcastle at approximately 10.30.

You will be aware, however, that there are other ways of referring to the future than by using the future tense. You could as naturally and correctly say, 'Our coach *is going to leave* at 5 o'clock' or 'Our coach *leaves* at 5 o'clock.' These are largely interchangeable, but there are slight differences in the way they might be used:

* *is going to leave* is the least formal;
* *will leave* may have a suggestion of intent: if you want to imply that latecomers will be left behind, *will* is the right word;
* *leaves* would definitely be used if you were referring to a regular service, every day or every week.

Future in the past bears the same relationship to the future as past perfect does to perfect and its form is like the future, but using *would* and *should* with the basic infinitive:

> Daniel *told* (past) Natalie that she *would get* (future in the past) the job.

What Daniel actually said was, 'You *will get* the job', a statement in the future tense made in the past.

Active and passive voice

The form of the verb is dictated by the **voice** as well as the tense. So far we have considered the **active voice** only; each of these tenses has an equivalent in the **passive voice**. It is not advisable in the interests of good style to make excessive use of the passive voice: it can be cumbersome and lack sharpness and precision. However, there are times when it is an essential means of expression.

Fortunately the names of the two voices are clear indicators of their meanings. In general use *active* means 'working' or 'energetic'; *passive* means 'suffering the action'. These are exactly their grammatical meanings. Normally the subject of a sentence is the person or thing doing an action or being described or identified. Sometimes, when using a transitive verb, we wish to feature the person or thing suffering the action – and this is when we employ the passive voice:

The left-winger *scored* the second goal. (active)
The second goal *was scored* by the left-winger. (passive)
The news *shocked* everyone in the village. (active)
Everyone in the village *was shocked* by the news. (passive)

Sometimes the doer of the action (identified by *by* in the above examples) is not identified at all, and sometimes not even known:

When I left my car at the station, the radio *was stolen*.
I found that all the mess *had been cleared* away.

The form of the passive voice consists of the auxiliary verb *to be* (in whatever tense is required), plus the past participle of the verb. Remember that the past participle is also used in the perfect tense, but with the auxiliary *to have*:

The window cleaner *has broken* his wrist. (perfect tense active)
It was when he fell off the ladder that his wrist *was broken*
    (simple past tense passive)

Subjunctive mood

The normal form of finite verbs is the **indicative** mood, dealing mainly with things that were, are or will be, though in conditional tenses there is movement towards the possible and the predictive. The **subjunctive** mood never deals with matters whose occurrence is definite, solely those that are ordered, doubtful or wished for.

If you have studied another language, it is quite possible that you have encountered a full set of subjunctive tenses equivalent to the indicative. It is, however, debatable whether English ever embraced the subjunctive to that extent and what remains is both slight in quantity and sometimes optional in use.

The present subjunctive

The form of the present subjunctive is identical with the basic infinitive form which means that, in most cases, it can be distinguished from the indicative only in the third person singular.

Infinitive/present subjunctive	Present indicative	
leave	I/you/we/they leave	He/she/it leaves
try	I/you/we/they try	He/she/it tries
but be	I **am**/you/we/they **are**	He/she/it is

All the uses of the present subjunctive suggest **a possibility**, **an intention** or **a wish**. Probably the most common is the construction based on words like *insist*, *request* and *demand*:

> I *insist* that he *leave* the meeting.
> Mr Ahmed *requested* that the committee *examine* his difficulty.
> You have ignored *my demand* that he *be* severely reprimanded.

Note that this form (the present) is also used in the past, as in the last two examples.

The past subjunctive

This has almost totally disappeared, existing solely in the use of the word *were*. Since this is the plural (and second person singular) of the simple past indicative, it means that the past subjunctive exists as a separate form only in the first and third person singular of the verb *to be*. Increasingly this tends to be replaced by *was*, especially in informal English, but the distinction between the two is useful. The subjunctive can be used in such cases as:

Suppose I *were* to offer you an increase...
If only he *were* happier at school...
I would rather she *were* left at home.

Imperative mood

The final type of finite verb need not detain us long, but should be noted. The imperative is used for commands and is the same in form as the indicative (and therefore, incidentally, the present subjunctive):

Stand up straight! *Leave* the building immediately!

The imperative can, of course, be more polite:

Please *stack* the plates over here.
Bring me your report if you have time.

A sort of imperative can even spread to the first person:

Let's drive down to visit Sinead.

You will note that the imperative is the only form of finite verb that operates without a subject. Normally a noun or pronoun expresses the doer of an action or the person/thing involved in the situation. With the imperative the subject is implied: it is *you*, the person or animal being addressed. 'Sit down!' effectively means '(You) sit down!'

Non-finite (non-tensed) verbs: the infinitive

A non-finite verb has no firm link to a period of time, cannot take a subject and therefore cannot be the main verb of a sentence or clause. The **infinitive** is the basic form of the verb, existing as a single word or following *to*. It is the form by which you identify the verb (*to be*, *to have*, etc.); you would never give the 'name' of a verb as 'being' or 'had'. Also the infinitive, as explained above, is frequently used with auxiliary and modal verbs.

In its own right the infinitive is used to form phrases which can be used as noun or adjectival phrases. Let us analyse four examples using the phrase *to pass the examination*:

> To pass the examination *is very easy*.
> *I wanted* to pass the examination.
> To pass the examination, *you must revise very thoroughly*.
> *I do not know how* to pass the examination.

The first two sentences are **noun phrases** – the first the subject of the sentence, the second the object of the verb *wanted*. If you find it difficult to envisage these as noun phrases, just consider nouns that might replace the infinitive phrase: 'English is very easy' or 'I wanted *my certificate*'. The third and fourth examples show the infinitive phrase with an adverbial function, in the second case dependent on the preposition *how*.

An infinitive can also be used in a common construction relating to the action that the *object* of the sentence is performing or might perform. This sounds contradictory as the object is the 'done-to' part of the sentence, but all becomes clear with the following examples:

> The children watched *the birds* (object) *fly* (infinitive) overhead.
> I saw *three ships* (object) *come* (infinitive) sailing in.

With verbs like *want*, *ask*, *advise*, *persuade* and *allow*, the *to* form of the infinitive is used:

> She wanted *me* (object) *to go* (infinitive) to the party.

The Prime Minister persuaded *the Cabinet* (object) *to accept* (infinitive) the cuts.

Past infinitives

Just as participles have past and present forms which do not in themselves determine the tense, there exists a **past** (or **perfect**) **infinitive** using the auxiliary *to have* + past participle:

to find/to gather/to avoid (present infinitive)
to have found/to have gathered/to have avoided (past infinitive).

The choice of which infinitive to use depends on the time relationships within the sentence, not on the time of the main event of the sentence. Compare the following examples:

To write my autobiography is a long job.
To have written my autobiography makes me very proud.
To write my autobiography required the assistance of a ghost writer.
To have written my autobiography seemed a major achievement at the time.

The first example is set totally in the present. The last one is set totally in the past: at some time in the past the writer had completed his/her autobiography and felt it was a major achievement. The most interesting examples are the second and third, both a mixture of present and past. The second sentence is in the present tense, but the past infinitive shows that now he/she has completed the task. The third sentence is in the simple past tense, but, as it refers to an event which was happening at that time, not one that had been completed, we use a present infinitive.

Participles and gerunds

Much more complex in their use are **past and present participles**. The form of the present participle causes no difficulty, consisting of *-ing* added to the infinitive, with the usual doubling of consonants after short vowels and removal of final silent e: *feel/feeling*, *pin/pinning, remove/removing*. The form of the past participle can give some problems: with possible confusion between past tense and past participle.

The problem with participles is that the same form can fulfil the functions of several parts of speech. We have already looked at one of the participle's verbal functions, creating tenses with the aid of auxiliary verbs: *are chasing, have eaten*, etc. Participles can also be used purely adjectivally. To add to the difficulty, the **gerund** (or verbal noun) has exactly the same form as the present participle. So the same form of the verb (the *-ing* form) can be used:

* in forming continuous tenses;
* in creating phrases where, like a verb, it attracts objects, complements and adverbial phrases;
* as an adjective;
* as a noun (gerund).

Let us examine some of these functions, bearing in mind that one thing a participle cannot do on its own is join with a subject and take on a tense to form a sentence: in other words, **a participle** can do many things, but it **cannot become finite**.

Verbal uses of participles and gerunds

Participles are frequently found in **participial phrases**, for example:

skating on the lake
defeated by a better opponent
revising for examinations
debating the future of transport
shocked by his apparent callousness

These can function as various types of phrase:

Skating on the lake, the minister made a splendid sight.
    (adjectival phrase with participle)
Skating on the lake has been banned because of thin ice.
    (noun phrase with gerund)

Josie is *revising for her examinations*. (adjectival phrase – with participle – as complement – or present continuous tense)
Revising for her examinations makes Josie irritable.
(noun phrase with gerund)
Defeated by a better opponent, I conceded the frame.
(adjectival phrase with participle)

In adjectival phrases care needs to be taken with the **dangling participle** (otherwise termed 'hanging', 'misrelated' or 'unattached'). Place the participial phrase next to the noun being qualified:

'*Walking to the buffet car*, the train suddenly lurched and I fell over.'

The meaning is clear, but what this actually says is that the train was walking to the buffet car. The correct version would be something like: '*Walking to the buffet car*, I fell over when the train gave a sudden lurch.'

Participles as adjectives

The distinction between a participle, a participle used adjectivally and an adjective derived from a verb is often a subtle and perplexing one. How would you describe the following participles?

I've just seen a *terrifying* film.
After the earthquake struck, the villagers tried to avoid *falling* masonry.
Visiting friends in Scotland, we were struck by the beauty of the scenery.
Retreating, the army soon ran short of food.

Each of these is a participle, each modifies a noun or pronoun (*film*, *masonry*, *we*, *army*). Each could therefore be called a participle used adjectivally. However, we tend to see *terrifying* as an adjective and *falling* as a participle used adjectivally simply because we are so accustomed to use *terrifying* (like *charming*, *interesting* or *amazing*) on its own with a noun. Perhaps a test of whether a participle has become an adjective in its own right is whether we regularly modify it with an adverb of degree:

quite terrifying   *absolutely* charming   *very* interesting
totally amazing

In the final two examples we are more aware of the participle's verbal function. In the last case *The retreating army* would stress the adjectival function more than *Retreating, the army...*

Gerunds as nouns

The same situation applies as with participles. The gerund can be used to form a **noun phrase**: '*Eating people* (subject) is wrong' or 'I enjoy *cycling round the Lake District* (object)'. You might like to note that, as the first example proves, gerunds can take objects: *Eating* is the gerund, *people* the object of the gerund and *Eating people* the subject of the sentence.

However, these same verbal nouns can also be used on their own with the function of nouns:

Eating is forbidden in the library.
Cycling improves your health.

4

modifiers: adjectives and adverbs

It's helpful to use the more modern term, 'modifiers', alongside the older terms, because adjectives and adverbs are among the more misunderstood parts of speech. While it's correct to call a noun a 'naming word' and at least half-correct to call a verb a 'doing word', the traditional application of the term 'describing words' to adjectives is frankly misleading.

What adjectives do is to modify the meaning of a noun or pronoun. Sometimes this is by description, but this is not always the case. When narrowing the meaning of the noun 'book', 'that book' (non-descriptive) does the same job as 'the red book', so 'that', like 'red', is an adjective.

Another common misunderstanding is that adverbs simply describe verbs. Certainly they do that ('He drove *recklessly*'), but they can also modify the meaning of verbs, adjectives, other adverbs and even the whole sentence.

Types of adjective

It is not necessary to know all the terms for different types of adjective; indeed, you will often find inconsistency over the correct terms to use. It is, however, helpful to be reminded of some of the various kinds of adjective:

Descriptive

This is the obvious type of adjective: *red*, *tall*, *violent*, *obsequious*, as long a list as you care to make. The only point to remember is that not all adjectives are describing words.

Demonstrative

Adjectives can simply demonstrate or point out which one you are referring to: *that* book, *this* summer, *those* flowers. These same words are **demonstrative pronouns** and current practice is always to refer to them as such, but traditional grammar makes a valid distinction. Used with a noun they are adjectives; used on their own, they are pronouns. 'Do you stock *this* (demonstrative adjective) magazine?' 'No, but *these* (demonstrative pronoun) might interest you.'

Possessive

According to traditional grammar, such examples as '*my* friend', '*your* ticket' and '*their* luggage' are possessive adjectives. Like demonstrative adjectives, they are now often considered as **pronouns**.

Numerical

The **cardinal** numbers (*one, two, three,* etc.) can be nouns ('the score was 3–1' or 'Flight Number 5034') or adjectives ('She had a choice of two cars' or 'a majority of 507 votes'). The **ordinal** numbers (*first, second, third,* etc.) tend to be adjectives. In addition to the actual numbers, there are other adjectives of **quantity** like *few*, *many* and *several*.

Interrogative/exclamatory

There are several words that can be used with many different functions, two of which are to join nouns in asking questions (**interrogative**) or making exclamations. You do not need to know these terms, but should be able to identity *which* and *what* as adjectives in the following: *Which* bus goes to the town centre?/*What* time is it?/*What* stupidity to expect me to believe that!/*What* sharp eyes you have!

Definite and indefinite articles

The definite (*the*) and indefinite articles (*a/an*) are a category of their own, usually classed nowadays as belonging to **determiners**, but in older grammar books they will be found under **adjectives**.

Factual

Some adjectives simply identify the noun without actually describing it: the *last* bus, *new* regulations, the *top* floor. These are not necessarily a separate category, but you need at least to remember to give the word 'descriptive' a wide definition.

The role of adjectives

The function of adjectives is to **modify or qualify a noun or pronoun**. A common placing for an adjective or adjectives is before the noun:

a *sunny* day	*three new* players	the *last* bus
red herrings	*this bold new* initiative	

They can be placed after the noun: this can sound old-fashioned and/or poetic, but can work well when you have a list of adjectives or an adjective phrase:

The tourist, *confused, penniless* and *demoralized*, asked for help.

There are limits to the situations in which an adjective can qualify a pronoun. In most of the examples above, if we replace the noun with a pronoun, the use of an adjective becomes impossible. References to *the last it* or *three new they* simply sound absurd. Following a pronoun with an adjective phrase, however, is possible, if frequently a little awkward:

I, *too short to see the procession*, could hear the cheering.

The most natural use of an adjective to modify a pronoun occurs when the words are separated from each other:

She realized the bus had gone and, *cold*, *wet* and *miserable*, prepared for a long wait.

Adjectival use of other parts of speech

You will sometimes find that other parts of speech are used adjectivally, in particular, nouns and the participle form of verbs. How, then, should you refer to these: as nouns/verbs or as adjectives? Again it is a matter of common sense. Look at the following examples:

fish shop   *street* corner   *cricket* ball   *nature* reserve

All the words in italics are clearly nouns, but they are being used to modify other nouns, the normal role of an adjective. In the first example, for instance, given the noun *shop*, we need more information: *large*, *new*, *prosperous* and *empty* (all adjectives) could give us information, but so could the nouns *fish*, *antiques*, *clothes* and *sports*. In these cases it is better to refer to these as 'nouns used adjectivally' rather than try to redefine them as adjectives.

A participle is the form of the verb lacking specific reference to subject and time. Words like *lying* and *running* (present participles) and *written* and *fallen* (past participles) attach themselves to nouns or other verbs to achieve their meaning. (Remember, though, that many verbs end in -*ed* both in the past tense and as past participles, so *attacked* or *laughed*, for instance, can be either.) Phrases like 'the *running* man' and 'the *fallen* tree' show participles being used in an adjectival role. Again it is sensible to refer to them in that way, not as adjectives. On the other hand, most people would accept words like *fascinating*, *charming*, *scared* and *delighted* as adjectives simply because of the frequency of their use as such. And, though dictionaries may list the verb *deject* as meaning *depress*, in reality *dejected* now exists only as an adjective.

The difference between adjectives and adverbs

The functions and form of adjectives and adverbs are very similar. In most cases the adverb consists of the adjective with -*ly* added (*beautiful/beautifully*); this will be considered in more detail later. Their roles in the sentence are to act as modifiers, adapting or intensifying the meaning of other words. Adjectives qualify nouns and pronouns; **adverbs** primarily qualify **verbs** (and this similarity in names makes the difference between adjectives and adverbs easy to remember).

Intelligent and *foolish* are words of opposite meaning, but there is no guarantee that intelligent people will not act foolishly. Similarly someone whom we could not describe as intelligent will display surprising acuteness of mind on some occasions. Thus there is a considerable difference between the word we might use to describe someone (an adjective describing a noun) and the word we might use for what he/she did on one occasion (an adverb describing a verb):

Mr Barwell proved an *intelligent* Managing Director over a ten-year period.
Mr Barwell acted *foolishly* in not foreseeing the slump in sales.

These sentences are not contradictory. The adjective, *intelligent*, accurately describes Mr Barwell; the adverb, *foolishly*, accurately describes what he did or failed to do on one occasion. If we add, 'His Deputy responded more *intelligently* to the situation', we are not necessarily implying the Deputy's general intellectual superiority.

Some cars are fast; some are not. However, even the fast cars go slowly at some times: a Formula One car in the pits or a sports car in a traffic jam on the M25. So, when you write, 'The car was moving *slowly* (adverb)', that is not the same as referring to a '*slow* (adjective) car'. This is the essential difference between adjectives and adverbs.

The form of adverbs

When formed from adjectives, adverbs nearly always add -*ly*. However, matters are not totally simple. You must remember that *well* is the adverb from *good*, for instance, and make sense of those adjectives that end in -*ly*: e.g. *lovely*, *ugly*, *gingerly*. When turned into adverbs, *lovely* becomes *lovelily* while *gingerly* stays the same and *ugly* lives up to its name with the logical, but odd-looking, *uglily*.

The rules governing the addition of -*ly* are mostly fairly straightforward, though subject to exceptions:

* Adjectives ending in *ll* simply add -*y* so that the adverbs are equivalent to those formed from adjectives ending in single *l*: *full* and *frightful* become *fully* and *frightfully*.
* As is common practice in English, a final *y* following a consonant is transformed into *i* before the addition of the ending: *dry/drily*, *gloomy/gloomily*, etc. The most common exceptions are *shyly* and *slyly*. Oddly there is at least one case where a final *y* following a vowel is changed in the same way: *gay/gaily* is, however, an exception.
* Adjectives ending in -*e* are subject to change. Words ending in -*le* after a consonant usually just change the final *e* to *y*: *subtle/subtly*, *agreeable/agreeably*, etc. In cases where a final *e* follows a vowel it is usually omitted: *eerie/eerily*, *true/truly*, etc. There are exceptions to both these rules, with, for instance, *whole* dropping the *e* (*wholly*) without being in either of these categories. In the case of words like *sole* and *vile* the adverb form is normal: *solely/vilely*.
* Perhaps the most confusing change is that most adjectives ending in -*ic* form the adverb by -*ally*: *basic/basically*,

characteristic/characteristically, etc. In cases where
the adjective can have either an *-ic* or an *-ical* ending,
the adverb always ends *-ically*: *comic*(*al*)/*comically*,
geographic(*al*)/*geographically*. Beware of *public/publicly*
and note that the adverb from *frantic* can be either *franticly*
or *frantically*.

* There are, of course, very many words that exist only as
  adverbs, not as formations from adjectives. Many of
  these are extremely common words: *here*, *there*, *soon*,
  very, *quite*, *again*, *today*, *tomorrow*, *however*, *therefore*, etc.
  There are also words like *before* and *on* that can function as
  adverbs and prepositions.

* Finally, there is a group of adverbs which have exactly the
  same form as the related adjectives: e.g. *hard*, *full*, *fast*, *only*
  and *long*. Compare:

  - 'His *hard* (adjective) work paid off' and 'He worked *hard*
    (adverb)'.
  - 'A *full* (adjective) theatre is always welcome' and
    'He hit me *full* (adverb) on the nose'.
  - 'I caught the *fast* (adjective) train' and 'She drove too *fast*
    (adverb)'.
  - 'She remains my *only* (adjective) rival' and 'It is *only*
    (adverb) right to obey'.
  - 'It's been a *long* (adjective) time' and 'I'd *long* (adverb)
    expected it'.

The uses of adverbs

The most widely used function of the adverb is modifying the
verb, but adverbs have many other uses:

Modifying adjectives

Though adjectives themselves are modifying or qualifying
nouns, we frequently add an adverb to intensify or describe the
adjective. For instance, the original phrase might refer to an
'*efficient* (adjective) manager', but not all efficient managers hit

the same level of efficiency or do it with the same style, so we might wish to add extra details:

Ms Thompson is an *extremely* efficient manager.
The manager is *fairly* efficient.
The manager is *usually* efficient.
Mr Briggs is a *briskly* efficient manager.
Mrs Green's management style is *calmly* efficient.

The first two statements show the degree of efficiency (there are many words we could have used, notably *very*). The next statement suggests some slight lack of consistency and the last two describe his/her manner (we could have chosen *relentlessly*, *gently*, *aggressively*, etc.). All the words in italics are adverbs.

Modifying other adverbs

This is essentially a similar function to modifying adjectives and the same 'specialist' adverbs are much used, especially those expressing degree: *very*, *quite*, *fairly*, *less*, etc. In the case of the sentence 'The actors performed *very well*', *well* is an adverb modifying the verb *performed*, *very* is also an adverb, but modifying *well*. There is no sense in which *very* can be seen as modifying the verb. You could easily replace *very* with *fairly* or *extremely* or a more descriptive adverb (not one of degree) such as *surprisingly*, *extraordinarily* or even *untypically*.

The position of the adverb in the sentence can make a difference. Let us examine two very similar sentences:

She *usually* drove her car *quickly*.
She drove her car *unusually quickly*.

In the first sentence both adverbs (*usually* and *quickly*) modify the verb (*drove*). *Quickly* is an adverbial complement and *usually* is placed before the verb and is telling us something about both that verb and its complement. In the second sentence *quickly* has the same function as before, but *unusually* has been placed in front of the adverb *quickly* which it is modifying: it is the speed, not the driving, that is unusual.

Modifying whole sentences or clauses

Sometimes adverbs relate to the whole sentence or clause. It is impossible to see them as relating to the verb only which is where they would have been placed in traditional analysis. Many of these 'whole-clause' usages have become rather meaningless: words like *actually*, *really* and *seriously* are often used as little more than punctuation, protestations of truth or appeals for attention:

> *Seriously*, I'm going to the pictures.
> *Actually* he's my next door neighbour.

In these cases the adverbs are simply insisting that the speaker is telling truth.

There are many adverbs that serve a much clearer function when modifying the whole sentence:

> *Incredibly* England gained a first innings lead. (suggesting that the whole statement is highly unlikely)
> *Therefore* we have decided to cut short your contract. (suggesting that the reasons have been given in previous sentences)
> *Indeed* I was hoping to see her myself. (suggesting a contradiction of previous implications or intensifying previous arguments)

The placing of adverbs

The fact that an adverb can modify different parts of the sentence means that it is necessary to take care where you place it. There are no specific rules about where an adverb modifying the verb should go, so that, in an uncomplicated statement with only one adverb, you could write:

> *Quickly* the secretary made a note of his name.
> or The secretary *quickly* made a note of his name.
> or The secretary made a note *quickly* of his name.
> or The secretary made a note of his name *quickly*.

Which sounds best? That is the only guide. However, there are cases where ambiguity can set in, with the adverb *only* a particular nuisance. What do these sentences mean?

He *only* wounded two of his victims.
He wounded *only* two victims.

In the first sentence *only* is connected to the verb *wounded* which it modifies: he only wounded them, he did not kill them, perhaps he killed some other victims. In the second sentence *only* has been linked to *two*, the adverb is modifying an adjective and the meaning is that the number wounded is low, not that they escaped something worse.

Or consider these sentences:

Clearly she gave evidence today.
She gave evidence *clearly* today.

In the first case the adverb modifies the whole statement. From something you have heard, it is certain that she gave evidence today: how clearly she gave evidence is not stated. In the second sentence the adverb modifies the verb *gave* and describes the quality of her performance in the witness box.

Adverbial phrases and clauses

As with adjectives, groups of words that may well not even contain an adverb can perform the function of adverbs: these are **adverbial phrases** and **adverbial clauses**, clauses containing a finite verb, phrases not. Traditional grammar books list something like ten or twelve different categories of adverbial clause and, while learning about adverbial clauses of concession is probably unnecessary, some awareness of these types conveys the wide range of adverbial functions.

Time

A major adverbial function is to state when the action occurred/will occur. Hence:

Yesterday my brother felt ill. (adverb)
In the evening my brother felt ill. (adverbial phrase)

When he arrived back from holiday, my brother felt ill.
(adverbial clause)

Place

As important as when the action took place is where it took place:

Our friends met us *there*. (adverb)
Our friends met us *at the station*. (adverbial phrase)
Our friends met us *where we asked them to* (adverbial clause)

Manner

This is the *How?* to go with the *Where?* and *When?*:

The meeting went *smoothly*. (adverb)
The meeting went *like clockwork*. (adverbial phrase)
The meeting went *just as we planned*. (adverbial clause)

Reason

The final question is, of course, *Why?*:

Inevitably the customers complained. (adverb)
The customers complained *in protest at the high prices*.
(adverbial phrase)
The customers complained *because the store increased prices*.
(adverbial clause)

Among other types of adverbial phrase or clause that you might wish to take note of are ones dealing with **comparison** (The Millennium Dome cost more *than had been planned*), **purpose/result** (often using *so that* or *in order to/that*), **contrast** or **concession** (usually with *though* or *although*) and **possibility** or **condition** (using words like *if* and *unless*).

5

function words: prepositions and conjunctions

Some analysts of language divide words into lexical words and function words. Lexical words have a meaning in their own right: a noun like *telephone* or a verb like *dance* creates an image in the reader's mind. The meaning of function words is defined by their relationship to other words. The difference between *on* and *under* is clear enough, but only comes to life when the reader knows what is on or under what.

Prepositions go before nouns and noun equivalents to link them to the rest of the sentence. Though they hardly have a meaning in their own right, their effect on the noun's relationship with the sentence is immense and correct use of prepositions is one of the key elements in idiomatic English.

Conjunctions join together different elements in a sentence and express the relationship between the various groups of words.

Prepositions

A preliminary warning that prepositions can also serve as other parts of speech is in order. Think of the words *down* or *on*:

I am waiting for the *down* train. (adjective modifying noun *train*)
The elm tree has blown *down*. (adverb modifying verb *blown*)
Sandra came running *down* the lane. (preposition linking *lane* to the sentence)
Can you find the *on* switch? (adjective modifying noun *switch*)
The Blackpool Illuminations will be turned *on* next week. (adverb modifying verb *turned*)
Tom kept treading *on* his partner's toes. (preposition connecting *his partner's toes* to the main statement)

Types of preposition

Prepositions can be divided into three categories:

1 **Simple prepositions:** The basic form of the preposition is usually a short word, often of one syllable, sometimes of two: in, *on*, *by*, *through*, *against*, *between*.
2 **Compound prepositions:** These are made up of two simple prepositions, sometimes joined into one word (*into*, *onto*), sometimes still two words (*out of* almost merges into one word, but there are also more cumbersome examples like *in between*).
3 **Complex prepositions:** A preposition with a single meaning may be made up of two or three words: *as well as*, *except for*, *in favour of*.

Prepositions with pronouns

The noun or pronoun following a preposition is technically the object of the preposition and is therefore in the objective case, but nouns, of course, remain unchanged. It is, however, important to remember that any pronoun so used must be in the objective case:

I sold my car to *him* yesterday.
She walked past *me* without speaking.
I've brought the children's presents for *them*.

This becomes less straightforward when there are two objects to a preposition, but the rule still applies:

> *Between you and me* I don't know what I'm going to do.
> Some old friends are here *with my husband and me*.

The grammatical construction remains the same whether or not there is an extra noun or pronoun. This error most often occurs with using *I* instead of *me*, perhaps because of a lingering sense that it is more polite, but simply remember that, because you would write or say 'for *me*' and 'to *me*' you must also use 'for *my wife and me*' and 'to *my friends and me*'.

The same applies to *who/whom*, which you might use in questions or subordinate clauses. In more formal style, you should write:

> Nick was the guest *with whom* we had the greatest difficulty.
> *At whom* exactly is this attack directed?

In informal English the pronoun can disappear (*Nick was the guest we had the greatest difficulty with*), but, if a pronoun is used, *whom* is, strictly speaking, correct. You will have to judge the context and your audience for yourself: you may feel that 'At *whom* is this attack directed?' sounds pompously formal in some settings.

Prepositions in dialect and slang

Prepositions are often affected by regional variations, though it must be said that some variant usages are very difficult to attribute to a specific region and may be more effectively seen as general colloquial forms. Look at the following examples:

> Have you seen the new shop *up* the village?
> I'm just going *down* the supermarket.
> It's more difficult nowadays for children to play out *on/of* a night.
> Becky's *out* the back making up the deliveries.

Some of these can be more economical usages than the 'correct' preposition. *Up* and *down* are used in place of *at*, *in* or *to*, but can also convey a sense of direction, though this is sometimes metaphorical, *up* being applied to a more important place. *Out* replaces a compound preposition, probably *out at*.

Of and *on* (which here are used instead of *at*) are sometimes interchangeable in colloquial English. Probably the form *some on 'em* for *some of them* is based around easier pronunciation; it is not normally heard with the full word *them*. On the other hand *of* can replace *on* in phrases like *of a Sunday*. You will notice a tendency in informal speech to add the indefinite article to prepositional phrases of time: *on a night* for *at night*, *of a Sunday* for *on Sunday*.

Though not necessarily completely national, all the above can be heard in many different areas. Other prepositional usages are more narrowly regional: *while* for *until* in parts of Yorkshire and Lancashire, *off of* in London and a whole series of localized variants on *to*, *at* or *in*. All these examples are normal and understandable in speech, but to be avoided in formal writing. Furthermore the variations demonstrate how difficult it can be to attribute a precise and fixed meaning to a preposition.

Some meanings of prepositions

A preposition serves to establish the relationship between a noun/pronoun/noun clause or phrase and the rest of the sentence. So, despite some blurring of margins of meaning, it is useful to examine some of these relationships:

Place and time

Oddly enough the same prepositions can serve for both:

I'll meet you *in* the evening *at* the restaurant.
I'll meet you *in* town *at* 8 o'clock.

In the first case *in* refers to time, *at* to place. In the second case the opposite is true. A few examples of other prepositions in this category are *outside*, *near*, *beyond* and *across* (place), *before*, *after* and *during* (time) and *by* (both – *by the door, by next week*).

Prepositions of place are perhaps the best examples of the power of the preposition in dictating meaning. Take the sentence, 'I put the parcel (*preposition*) the table' and think of the differences between using *by*, *on*, *under*, *next to*, *behind*, etc.

Possession

Among the most commonly used prepositions is *of*, but the idea of possession or belonging covers a wide field. Think of the differences in meaning between 'the first act *of* the play', 'built *of* brick', 'the symphonies *of* Beethoven', 'a picture *of* happiness' and '*of* dubious origins'.

Cause, reason, etc.

Obviously the compounds *because of* and *owing to* bulk large here, but there is also *through*, yet another preposition with widely diverse meanings: 'I lost the job *through* no fault of my own' (reason), 'Have you been *through* the Channel Tunnel?' (place), 'I stayed awake all *through* the night' (time).

Instrument of action

The prepositions *by* and *with* can indicate who or what did an action, particularly valuable with the passive voice (The Arts Centre was opened *by* the Mayor), but also in sentences such as 'I cut myself *with* a knife.'

Prepositions in regular constructions

Many nouns, verbs and adjectives regularly take set prepositions. You have an *aversion to* guilt which is *preferable to* being *ashamed of* your actions and you are to be *congratulated on* your *tendency to* retain *confidence in* yourself, *opposite to* many people today.

Inevitably there are some complications here. Many people say *different to* when the 'correct' form is *different from*. However, it is difficult to disapprove when *different to* was the accepted form in Victorian times and when the American *different than* is making inroads into English usage. For the moment, however, *different from* is safest.

Then there are words which take different prepositions depending on the connection being established. A number of *to/for* usages relate *to* a person, principle or institution *for* a particular reason or act: we might apologize *to* somebody *for* what we have done or be responsible *to* the management *for* one area of production.

Other interesting examples include:

* **inform of/on:** *Of* relates to the information given ('I have informed the police *of* the break-in'); *on* refers to incriminating someone ('Fortunately a member of the public informed *on* the criminal') or a general area of knowledge ('Keep me informed *on* the case').
* **sympathy for/with:** *With* is used for a sharing of opinions and feelings ('We have sympathy *with* the view that a new transport policy is essential'); *for* most often relates to a person and expresses sorrow rather than agreement ('Of course we feel sympathy *for* the victims').
* **free(dom) from/of/with:** *From* and *of* overlap somewhat, but *free from* is most often used of escaping an actual unpleasant situation (*free from* prison/poverty/pursuit) and *of* most often suggests the area in which the freedom operates (*freedom of* choice/conscience/religion). *Free with*, however, suggests unwarranted liberty: 'He made *free with* my hospitality.'
* **agree to/with:** Traditionally we are said to agree *to* a thing or *with* a person. This is not strictly true. If we agree *with* a person or principle or action, we think that it is a good thing. If we agree *to* a proposal, we accept that it will be put into practice, not quite the same: 'Although I *agree with* your plans for redevelopment, I cannot *agree to* the proposal to include them on next year's budget.'
* **authority on/over:** This relates to two different meanings of authority. It can mean someone very well informed ('Professor Butt is an *authority on* ancient Indian manuscripts') and a position of power ('In the colonial period European nations claimed *authority over* most of Africa').

Conjunctions

The function of conjunctions is to join together clauses into **compound** or **complex** sentences. The actual form of conjunctions is relatively simple. Two forms of conjunction exist: **co-ordinating conjunctions** and **subordinating conjunctions**. Co-ordinating conjunctions *conjoin* clauses which are equal or *co-ordinate*, most obviously in the case of the conjunction *and*:

I drove into town *and* met Mrs Ross.

Each half is equal; no attention is focused on one part at the expense of the other. When there is a different subject in the second half, some writers prefer to add a comma:

I drove into town, *and* the traffic was dreadful.

There are few co-ordinating conjunctions, each providing a very basic guide to the relationship between the two halves: *and* tells us nothing more than both halves took place, *but* implies that the second clause is a contrast, *so* suggests that it is predictable and *or* expresses alternatives:

The weather improved, *but* the game was called off.
The weather deteriorated, *so* the game was called off.
The weather must improve *or* the game will be called off.

Two final notes on co-ordinating conjunctions

This section deals particularly with conjunctions in their function of joining together clauses. However, *and*, *or* and *but* (as in 'slow, *but* sure') can also join together words or phrases. This is still regarded as a conjunctional usage. *So*, as in *so near and yet* (a less used conjunction) *so far*, can also be used as an adverb.

Over-use of *and* can be a weakness of style. *And* tells us nothing about the relationship between the units on each side of it, with resulting sloppiness of expression. Generally you should avoid more than one *and* (in its function of joining clauses) in a sentence without some deliberate reason. On the other hand, lists of clauses can be effectively dramatic or humorous, usually saving *and* for the final junction, just as in lists of words:

The saucepan was boiling over, the cat had a half-eaten chicken leg on the floor, the children's castle had collapsed all over the hallway, the milkman stood on the doorstep still waiting to be paid, *and* Mrs Merrick sat at the kitchen table engrossed in her latest Mills and Boon romance.

Subordinating conjunctions

Subordinating conjunctions not only link parts of a sentence, but have meanings, sometimes very precise meanings, of their own, in introducing subordinate clauses, usually **subordinate adverbial clauses**:

Time: *after, before, since, when, as, whenever*, etc.
Place: *where*
Manner: *as*
Reason: *because, as, since.*
Possibility: *if* (positive), *unless* (negative)
Contrast/concession: *though, although.*
Purpose/result: *(in order)(so) that* (positive), *lest* (negative)

That is also commonly used to introduce subordinate noun clauses: 'She told me that I must work harder.'

The function of subordinating conjunctions

These meanings make the function of subordinating conjunctions different from that of co-ordinating conjunctions.
The subordinating conjunction:
* connects together two clauses;
* dictates which one is the main focus of our attention;
* specifies the relationship of the other clause to that main clause.

If you take the two statements, *Judith finished reading her book* and *Judith came over for a coffee*, you can join them in many different ways, the most obvious and least interesting being by placing *and* in the middle. But what is the difference between the two following sentences?

> When Judith finished reading her book, she came over for a coffee.
>
> Before Judith came over for a coffee, she finished reading her book.

In terms of meaning, there is no difference, but the first example makes coming for a coffee the main statement and the second makes reading the book the centre of attention: *when* and *before* are subordinating conjunctions introducing the less important part (a **subordinate adverbial clause**). The choice of which is the most important clause helps indicate what is the theme of your narration. You might therefore expect the first example to continue '…She stayed for an hour and told me about her problems at work', whereas the second might go on to tell us about what the book was and how much she enjoyed it.

As well as directing our attention to one part of the sentence, the subordinating conjunction establishes a relationship between the clauses which may alter the whole meaning of the sentence. What does it tell us if we insert different conjunctions between *I won't go to the cinema*, and *There is a horror film showing*?

	unless	
	although	
I won't go to the cinema	*when*	there is a horror film showing.
	because	
	until	

Because and *although* suggest that you are referring to this week only: *because* means that you avoid horror films; *although* means that you would like to see the horror film, but don't wish to go for some other reason. The other three refer to your regular policy: *when* means that you refuse to watch horror films; *unless* that you watch nothing else; and *until* that you watch nothing else, but the cinema never shows them! By employing different subordinating conjunctions, you are thus able to comment on the characters and situation as well as effecting a grammatical junction.

6

phrases and clauses

The previous five chapters have dealt with the main parts of speech. Now it's time to examine how they fit together to make groups of words. Strictly speaking, this analysis of the structure of sentences is known as syntax, but it is convenient to consider it within the overall study of grammar.

In correct and formal English every sentence contains at least one clause. A clause is a group of words that contains a finite (tensed) verb and, in nearly every case, a subject which is a noun, pronoun or noun phrase or clause. This chapter explains the difference between main and subordinate clauses: a sentence may contain several subordinate clauses.

A phrase is a group of words which does the job of a specific part of speech: noun, verb, adverb or adjective. Having no finite verb, it has less independence than does a clause.

The difference between phrases and clauses

A phrase in normal parlance is any group of words combined together. Its meaning in grammatical terms is very similar, but with one exception: any group of words containing a finite verb, with subject either real or implied, is defined as a **clause**. A clause can be an entire sentence in itself or the main element of a longer sentence or an equal element in a sentence or a minor (**subordinate**) part of a sentence. Phrases and subordinate clauses function as a specific part of speech and are identified as such.

The builders start work tomorrow. (a sentence of one single clause)

Tomorrow the builders start work and I have to catch the early train to the office. (two equal clauses joined by *and*)

When the builders start work, I'll have to set the alarm for 7.00. (a subordinate clause functioning as an adverb)

Having the builders in is a nuisance. (a phrase functioning as a noun – subject)

A lorry *with a load of bricks* has arrived. (a phrase functioning as an adjective – modifying *lorry*).

How big is a phrase?

This is an unanswerable question. Although a clause contains a key element lacking in a phrase (a finite verb), a phrase can be much longer than a clause, as long as you like and your reader/listener will tolerate:

When summer comes... (clause)

In the months of July and August, with extended holidays from work, excursions to the seaside, foreign travel, long sunny days, Test matches and Wimbledon... (phrase)

Noun phrases

All phrases assume the functions of the part of speech they are identified with, so for noun phrases key functions include subject, object and complement of a sentence. A noun phrase will customarily include a noun or noun equivalent (pronoun or gerund).

Compare the two following sentences and you will see that the function is exactly the same as a single noun:

The photographer asked *all the tall men in the team* to stand at the back.
The photographer asked *Mark* to stand at the back.

Each is fulfilling the function of direct object of the verb *asked*.

Verb phrases

Quite simply those verbs consisting of more than one word because of the use of **auxiliary** and/or **modal verbs**, are referred to as **verb phrases**. The verbs are italicized in the following examples:

The big bay horse *led* the field.
The big bay horse *was leading* the field.

The second example may be referred to as a verb phrase – very straightforward, though it is as well to remember that verb phrases can be surprisingly long:

We had all thought that the coastguard *would have been trying to rescue* the crew since Monday.

Adjectival phrases

These can be divided into three categories:

1 **adjective phrases proper** which all grammar systems acknowledge as such. These usually use adjectives with extra modifiers (a *joyfully triumphant* expression, the *carefully restored* brickwork) or intensifiers (*very fine* lace, an *extremely dry* summer).
2 **participial phrases** which are now sometimes regarded as clauses, but according to traditional grammar are phrases. Remember that a participial (adjective) phrase and a gerund-based noun phrase may look identical; only the function makes a difference. '*Whistling a happy tune*

(gerund – noun phrase) can cheer you up'/'A nun *whistling a happy tune* (participle – adjective phrase) comes as a surprise.'

3 **prepositional phrases** which can be so termed because they are introduced by a preposition, but which can also be named according to the part of speech they replace. *In a bad mood* or *outside the gate* are prepositional phrases, but in the following examples they are used adjectivally: 'Mr Stevens *in a bad mood* was someone to avoid', 'The postman *outside the gate* refused to come in while the dog was loose'.

Adverbial phrases

A group of words which refers to such things as the time, manner, place and cause of the events in the sentence is an **adverbial phrase**. Of course many of these can be categorized as **prepositional phrases**, but if you look at the following examples you will see that they perform an adverbial function:

The painters came back from their dinner *fairly quickly*.
   (adverbial phrase of time consisting of two adverbs)
The painters came back from their dinner *in about half an hour*. (adverbial phrase of time/prepositional phrase)
Pirates were supposed to hide their treasure *extremely carefully*.
   (adverbial phrase of manner consisting of adverbs)
Pirates were supposed to hide their treasure *with extreme secrecy and cunning*. (adverbial phrase of manner/prepositional phrase)

Main clauses

Though we tend to use the term **grammar** for the form of interconnections between words, sentence construction, etc., the correct term for the organization of a sentence is **syntax**. The most important syntactical unit is the **main (or principal) clause**. All sentences have at least one, some sentences have a main clause and nothing else and it constitutes the smallest unit that makes syntactical sense on its own.

In defining the form of a main clause, traditional and contemporary terminology are in agreement to an unusual degree. Traditionally it consists of (parts in parentheses not always present):

subject	+	**predicate**
noun or noun	+	**verb (direct object or complement)**
equivalent		**(indirect object) (adverbial qualification)**

Subject and predicate

The **subject** is the doer of the action, the sufferer of the action in a passive sentence or the person/thing whose condition is being stated. Remember that, as the above section and the later section on **noun clauses** show, the subject can be extended through many words.

The **verb** similarly can be more than one word, with the use of auxiliaries. The only qualification necessary is that it must be a **finite (tensed)** verb. Interestingly the only case where the part of speech and part of the sentence/clause share an identical name, it is not difficult to recognize.

If the verb is **intransitive,** the predicate can stop there. If it is **transitive**, we need to follow it with a **direct object (objective complement)**, the person/thing who suffers the action. If it is a **verb of being**, we need to follow it with a **complement (intensive complement)** to complete the meaning. Thus the simplest forms of main clauses may be exemplified as follows:

> *The river* (subject) *flows* (predicate – verb only).
> *Mrs Beeton* (subject) *wrote a famous book* (predicate – verb + direct object).
> *Charles Dickens* (subject) *was a distinguished author* (predicate – verb + complement).

The indirect object

Though any of the nouns in a sentence may be accompanied with adjectives/adjective phrases, there are only two more parts (both optional) of the main clause: the **indirect object** and the **adverbial qualification**, both of which can be defined in terms of complements.

Some actions can have two different forms of object.
If you give a pound to a charity collector, whom or what is your
action done to: the pound or the collector? Both, of course, one
experiencing it directly, the other experiencing it indirectly by
receiving it. So, in the following sentence, *a pound* is the direct
object and *the collector* the indirect object:

> I gave the collector a pound.

Look at the following examples to reinforce your awareness
of the difference between **direct** and **indirect** objects:

> The RSPCA awarded *Susan* (indirect) *a medal* (direct).
> My wife sent *me* (indirect) *a message* (direct).
> He accidentally struck *his friend* (indirect) *a blow on the
> face* (direct).

The last example shows that the use of the word 'indirect' can
be misleading. If the sentence had read 'He struck his friend', *friend*
would have been the direct object.

Adverbial qualifications

These may take the form of single adverbs or adverbial phrases,
but the main distinction is between those that are necessary
to complete the sense of the verb (**adverbial complements**)
and those that simply add information to a verb whose sense
is complete. This information may possibly be essential to the
understanding of the sentence, but not to the completion of the
verb. Look at the slightly different functions of *in the corner*
(in all cases adverbial) in the following sentences:

> The table is *in the corner*.
> We placed the sideboard *in the corner*.
> He is quite happy *in the corner*.

In all the sentences the phrase is important, but only in the
first is it used as a complement. In the second it is an adverbial
qualification in a sentence where a transitive verb takes a direct
object (*sideboard*). In the third, the other example of a verb of
being, the adjectival *quite happy* serves as an intensive complement.

So perhaps we should look at two examples (the first a verb of doing, the second a verb of being) of a main clause presenting all the features possible:

> *Late every afternoon* (adverbial qualification) *the delivery man from the bakery* (subject, including adjectival modification) *brought* (verb) *the corner shop* (indirect object) *a supply of cakes* (direct object).
> *Councillor Pilkington* (subject) *will become* (verb) *Chairman of the Ways and Means Committee* (intensive complement) *next year* (adverbial qualification).

Main clauses as questions

All the above comments have been based on the **main clause as statement**. The essential structure remains unchanged for **questions**. Three very straightforward changes occur for questions:

1 If the verb is a single word, it must divide into two: *likes* into *does like*, *drive* into *do drive*, *found* into *did find*, etc.
2 The word order is then changed to place the subject after the first part of the verb. These two rules apply both when an interrogative word (*how*, *why*, *where*, etc.) is used and when the question is a simple one requiring a *Yes/No* answer.
3 The sentence ends with a question mark. Therefore '*I found the tickets in the sideboard drawer*' becomes:

> Where *did you find* the tickets?

or

> *Did you find* the tickets in the sideboard drawer?

Commands and exclamations

In the case of a **command** the subject of the main verb customarily disappears; the doer is the person addressed:

> The staff (subject) always locked the shop door at 6 o'clock. (statement)

Lock the shop door at 6 o'clock. (command with *you* implied as subject)

Exclamations are of no real grammatical importance. They fall into two categories:

1 Some phrases (*Heavens above! Goodness gracious me!* etc.) or even single words (*Jiminy! Crivvens!*) exist as 'set' exclamations, some with no life of their own outside this. These operate outside the general syntax of the piece. All you need to remember is that, from a punctuation point of view, they are normally regarded as full sentences and the exclamation mark is followed by a capital letter. (Some authors, understandably, go their own way on this.)

2 Anything (except a question) can become an exclamation and the punctuation mark simply tells us the tone of voice or emphasizes the drama/surprise/comedy of the situation. *Bring me my brief case at once!* suggests an angry boss or a dilatory employee, while *Aunt Louisa walked into the room!* makes sense if the assembled company thought she was stuck in a snowdrift in the Cairngorms or had just been slandering her character.

Subordinate clauses

Traditionally subordinate clauses, like phrases, bear the name of the parts of speech whose function they fulfil. The essential functions of a noun are to act as subject, object (direct or indirect) or intensive complement. So **a noun clause** is any group of words containing a finite verb that fulfils one of these functions. In just the same way a group of words containing a finite verb and modifying a noun can be seen as an **adjective clause**. Superficially they can look very similar:

The umbrella *that I left at the airport* was never found.
   (adjective clause modifying *umbrella*)
That I left in a hurry shows how boring the meeting was.
   (noun clause – subject)

Didn't you know *that I left my umbrella behind*? (noun clause – direct object of *did know*)

The reason I got out of the car park so easily was *that I left early*. (noun clause – intensive complement relating to subject 'reason')

Relative clauses

A different method of categorizing these subordinate clauses refers to the means by which they are linked to the rest of the sentence. Those clauses introduced by a **relative pronoun** (*who*, *which*, *that*, etc.) or a phrase including one (*by whom*, *for which*, etc.) are commonly called **relative clauses**.

However, though a majority of noun and adjective clauses are introduced by relative pronouns, many are introduced by **subordinating conjunctions** and may take exactly the same form as **adverbial clauses**, though functioning as nouns or adjectives.

Let us take, for example, the clause, *Where I spent my holidays*. Beginning with the subordinating conjunction *where*, it looks like an adverbial clause of place – and so it can be. Now let us examine three entirely different usages of the clause:

Where I spent my holiday, there is a wide bay with hotels and casinos surrounding it.

How do you know *where I spent my holiday*?

The village *where I spent my holiday* is in the foothills of the Alpujarras.

The first is the predicted adverbial clause of place, but what of the other two? The second is the object of *know* and thus a **noun clause**. The third modifies the noun *village* and is an **adjective clause**. Examine the following examples referring to time:

When the fog lifts, we shall be able to see the mountains. (adverbial)

When the fog lifts is the best time to cross. (noun)

The time *when the fog lifts* is a matter of guesswork. (adjective)

Appositive noun clauses

The form of appositive clauses is very like that of relative clauses, but rather than relating to or modifying the noun, an appositive clause stands **in apposition to** it; in other words, it is equivalent in grammatical function and, to an extent, in meaning, referring to the same person or thing. Examples of nouns and phrases in apposition are:

Mr Bromilow, the Town Clerk
George Eliot, the famous Victorian novelist
the first supersonic airliner, Concorde

In the each case the name and the phrase refer to the same person or thing. Two phrases can work in the same way:

The first speaker, the local secretary of the Townswomen's Guild.

Appositive clauses maintain this balance of equivalents:

I've just heard *the news* (1) *that the supermarket is closing down* (2 – appositive clause).
My parents always gave me *strict instructions* (1) *that I should be careful crossing the road* (2 – appositive clause).

In each case 1 and 2 are equivalent; in the first example the sentence would read smoothly with either the noun or the appositive clause omitted. Compare that with the relative clause:

I've just heard the news *that Chris shouted up to me.*

The relative clause is an adjectival clause modifying the noun *news* which is essential to the meaning of the sentence.

Adverbial clauses

Earlier in this chapter the account of main clauses referred to adverbial qualifications. If these consist of single adverbs or adverbial phrases, they are part of the main clause. On the other hand the same function can be taken on by a clause which then becomes a **subordinate adverbial clause**. In traditional grammars the list of possible types of adverbial clause can be alarming and unnecessary, but the following list (which could be applied also to adverbial phrases) is probably helpful and sufficient:

> time, place, manner, reason, purpose/result, possibility/condition, contrast/concession.

Time, place and manner

These answer the big questions *When? Where? How?*. Adverbial clauses of **place** are usually introduced by the subordinating conjunction *where* (*wherever* can also be used, as can the almost archaic *whither* and *whence*, meaning *to where* and *from where*). Adverbial clauses of **time** may well use *when*, but there is a much greater range of possibilities: not only *whenever*, but also *after*, *before*, *as*, *since*, *whil(e)(st)*, etc:

> *Where the children used to play*, you can still see the swing.
> I will put the box *wherever you want it*.
> *As the ship lurched from side to side*, we all held on tightly.
> Mrs Jordan used to shudder *whenever she passed the scene of the crime*.
> *Before Sarfraz let the building to us*, he used it as a workshop.

Adverbial clauses of **manner** differ in that the key question word (*How?*) is not used as an introductory subordinating conjunction. Usually such clauses are introduced by *as* or some phrase using *as*:

> Jeremy climbed into the racing car *as if he had been doing it all his life*.
> The results came out *as I expected*.

Of course, the versatile *as* can also convey time or reason. You may also be puzzled by the statement that *how* is not used to introduce adverbial clauses: surely *how* can be a subordinating conjunction? True, but the clauses it introduces are *noun clauses*:

> *How it got here* is a mystery. (subject)
> The police inquiry established *how the weapon was concealed*. (direct object)

Reason and purpose/result

These answer the questions *Why?* and *To what effect?*
For **reason** you use the subordinating conjunctions *because* and
(again) *as* and *since*. Clauses of **purpose** and **result** it is hardly
necessary to separate: both deal with consequences and both use
so that (*purpose* also uses *in order that*). Clauses of **purpose** imply
more intent, but the distinction is not one to worry about. Both
clauses of reason and clauses of purpose/result deal with Event B
happening because of Event A. A subordinate clause of **reason** deals
with Event A and accompanies a main clause telling of Event B.
A clause of **purpose/result** deals with Event B and accompanies
a main clause telling of Event A. Let us take the example of a river
flooding (Event A) and a village being cut off (Event B). There are
two opposite ways of expressing the same idea:

> The village was cut off *because the river flooded*. (reason)
> The river flooded *so that the village was cut off*.
> (purpose/result)

The following example implies more intent (**purpose**):

> Christina worked hard *so that she could pass her examinations*.
> (purpose/result)
> *Because Christina worked so hard*, she passed her
> examinations. (reason)

There is a negative subordinating conjunction expressing
purpose or result: *lest*. This sounds very formal and we often prefer
the normal *so that* with an added negative, though it is a longer
construction. The two following examples mean exactly the same
thing:

> We need to maintain the sea wall *lest there should be* (or *is*)
> widespread flooding.
> We need to maintain the sea wall *so that there will not be*
> widespread flooding.

Possibility/condition and contrast/concession

The other main forms of adverbial clause (traditionally known
as clauses of **condition** and **concession**) are used in sentences

dealing with things that might happen and things that contrast with each other. If you find the terms **possibility** and **contrast** more easily memorable, there is no reason why you should not use those instead. The subordinating conjunctions *if* and *unless* introduce **clauses of condition**, providing the positive and negative forms of what might happen:

If the Government calls an election (a possibility expressed in positive terms), the result is hard to predict.
Unless the Government calls an election (a possibility expressed negatively), the new Public Order Bill will be passed this year.

The subordinating conjunctions *though* and *although* introduce clauses (of **concession**) which are in contrast to the main clause. The co-ordinating conjunction *but* can perform the same function, but *though* and *although* focus attention on what is important in the sentence while *but* links equal halves. Let us imagine that we have two pieces of information about an employee: she has worked for the company for only a year and she is a senior manager. The short service and the senior position are in contrast, but the relationship can be expressed in at least two different ways:

Though she is a senior manager, she has only a year's experience.
Though she has only a year's experience, she is a senior manager.

Each uses the same information to give a different insight. The main statement in the first is that she is junior in time: in other words, although she is your boss, do not expect her to remember the supply problems you had three years ago or that scandal with the Managing Director and his last-but-two secretary. The second concentrates on her senior position: it is simple admiration or envy or a warning to the listener to be respectful even though he has more years' service.

7

kinds of sentence

It is important to understand how different types of sentence are structured. Obviously such matters as paragraphing are important in written English, but poor paragraphing is simply clumsy or unhelpful: the ability to construct a sentence correctly is essential in writing correct English.

There are three main types of sentence. The simple sentence is just one main clause, though it is worth remembering that even a simple sentence may be complicated by the use of many phrases. Joining two or more clauses together as co-ordinate clauses produces a compound sentence. The greatest care, however, has to be taken with the complex sentence in which one or more subordinate clauses support the main clause. This enables subtler relationships between the various parts of the sentence.

A fourth form is the hybrid compound-complex sentence where more than one main clause is joined by one or more subordinate clauses.

Simple sentences

A simple sentence is exactly what it says: simple in that it is a single item as well as being an easy concept to understand. A simple sentence consists of **one clause only**, the main clause. It can be a statement, question or command and is always terminated by a full stop, question mark or exclamation mark.

Though a single item, a simple sentence is by no means always short. The subject may be modified by an adjective **phrase** (*the man in the iron mask*) or can consist of multiple subjects (*Athos, Porthos, Aramis and D'Artagnan*). The verb can quite easily become a verb phrase (*may be about to start*). If the verb is transitive, there is scope for direct and indirect object, both capable of as much development as the subject. There is no reason why adverbial qualifications should not multiply, covering time, place, etc. This complicated sentence is a **simple sentence**:

> In the 19th century the Count of Monte Cristo and the Three Musketeers presented images of romantic heroism to the eager novel reader via the fictions of Alexandre Dumas.

The sentence begins with one adverbial phrase (time – *In the 19th century*) and ends with another (manner – *via the fictions of Alexandre Dumas*). If the verb (*presented*) is one word only, the multiple subject preceding it consists of nine words. Fairly lengthy objects follow: *images of romantic heroism* (direct) and *to the eager novel reader* (indirect). Why, then, do we call the sentence simple? There is only one finite verb, all the other additions are merely phrases and a simple structure underlies the verbiage:

> subject – verb – direct object – indirect object – adverbial qualification

Compound sentences

If you put together two or more main clauses (**co-ordinate clauses**) in one sentence, that is known as a **compound sentence**.

Alternatively two co-ordinate clauses can be said to make a **double sentence**, more than two a **multiple sentence**. The normal way of forming a compound sentence is to place a **co-ordinating conjunction** between the clauses:

> The doctor suspected flu, *but* it was only a bad cold.
> The waiter will bring your soup *or* you can collect it from the buffet.
> The public address system began paging Walter, *and* he soon came into sight.
> The *Three Musketeers* books sold well *and* made Alexandre Dumas very famous.

You will, incidentally, note differences of practice in terms of whether or not to include a comma before the conjunction. A comma is usually required before *but*, but not *or*. *And* is subject to more variation: the wisest policy is never to include a comma when the second clause uses the same subject (usually not repeated) as the first, as in the final example where *The Three Musketeers books* is the subject of both clauses. If the subject changes, it is sometimes preferable to include a comma.

Compound sentences can be more than two clauses long, but normally it is clumsy to have more than one *and*. Although separating two clauses by a comma with no conjunction is usually to be avoided, a series of co-ordinate main clauses can be treated like a list:

> The electricity came back on, the fire began to warm up *and* the kettle started boiling.

This is a perfectly acceptable sentence, although 'The electricity came back on, the fire began to warm up' would have required *and* or a different punctuation mark.

It is, of course, quite usual to have compound sentences using more than two co-ordinate clauses and a variety of conjunctions:

> The kitchen was well equipped *and* the cook took pride in her work, *but* Mr Jephcoat usually ate a sandwich *or* asked them to prepare a small salad.

Compound sentences without co-ordinating conjunctions

As already stated, a comma is not sufficient to separate two co-ordinate main clauses without the use of a conjunction. However, using a **colon** or **semicolon** can create compound sentences without a conjunction.

A **semicolon** is used for those situations where a comma seems too slight and a full stop too complete a pause. In terms of compound sentences, this is of assistance when you are faced with two separate statements which are so closely linked that you do not wish to start a new sentence (see Chapter 8).

The **colon** has a more specific function. When the second main clause explains or enlarges on the first, the colon is the necessary punctuation (see Chapter 8).

How do you merge two statements?

Let us examine these two statements, two separate sentences, and decide how to make them one:

> The vicar was ill last Christmas.
> The special family service was cancelled.

You could, of course, use a co-ordinating conjunction (*and*, *so*) to form a compound sentence and, as the next section will show, a rather more interesting method is to choose a subordinating conjunction (*because*, *when*, etc.) to form a **complex sentence**.

There are ways, however, of merging the two into **one simple sentence**:

* Refine one of the sentences into a noun/noun phrase:
  * The vicar's illness last Christmas caused the special family service to be cancelled.
* Create an adverbial phrase (of reason or time):
  * Owing to/because of/after the vicar's illness last Christmas the special family service had to be cancelled.
* Create a non-finite/participial clause:
  * With falling ill last Christmas, the vicar had to cancel the special family service.

Note that it is essential to place *the vicar* next to the participial clause.

Complex sentences: choosing the main clause

A complex sentence is defined as one containing a main clause and one or more subordinate clauses. The first stage is to decide what constitutes the main clause. What differences can you find in the following pairs of sentences? In each the main clause is italicized:

A Though I thought Emily was a suitable candidate, *Mrs Tankard disagreed.*
Though Mrs Tankard disagreed, *I thought Emily was a suitable candidate.*
B Where the old Fire Station used to be, *the Khans have opened a nursery.*
The old Fire Station used to be where the Khans have opened a nursery.
C When the town centre has a bit more life, *new shops will open.*
The town centre will have a bit more life when some new shops open.

In every pair each sentence contains the same information, but the emphasis is quite different. In A we receive a lower opinion of Emily in the first sentence because Mrs Tankard's opinion is the point of focus, whereas the second sentence pays more heed to the speaker/writer's more favourable opinion. In B the listener knows the whereabouts of a different place (the Khans' nursery or the old Fire Station) in each sentence and is being told about the other place. In C it is a question of whether new shops will enliven the town centre or a lively town centre attract new shops – the sequence of improvement varies from sentence to sentence. A choice between main and subordinate clauses is a choice of focus for your complex sentence.

Subordinate adverbial clauses

An adverbial clause is any statement containing a finite verb and relating to the action or state of the main clause. As such there is no rule about the placing of an adverbial clause in the sentence:

After I have been shopping, I might find time for some gardening.
I might find time for some gardening *after I have been shopping*.

There is absolutely no difference between the meaning of these sentences. Furthermore adverbial clauses frequently multiply in a complex sentence, placed at various stages of the main clause; for instance:

When Mrs Johnson visited the hospital (1), she always drove to Car Park D *unless the space was already full* (2), *as she could easily walk to the ward from there* (3).

Adverb clause 1 (time), 2 (negative possibility) and 3 (reason) all tell us something about the main statement: where Mrs Johnson parked. In theory the order of these clauses could change, although the order employed here is the most logical.

Subordinate noun clauses

The integration of noun clauses into a complex sentence differs from that of adverbial clauses. An adverbial clause has many functions relative to the entire sentence (commenting on the time, place, possibility, etc.) or the action. A noun clause takes the place of a key unit of the sentence, the **subject** or some form of **complement**: direct object, indirect object or intensive complement.

The first difference that you may notice is one of punctuation. The noun clause becomes an integral part of the flow of the main clause: the essential movement from subject to verb and (usually) on to some form of completion of the verb. Therefore a noun clause is seldom separated from the rest of the sentence by a comma.

Think of a complex sentence of a mere 12 letters that is familiar to all as the motto of the SAS and the title of various books, films and articles:

Who dares wins.

Who dares is a noun clause meaning a daring person or someone who takes risks and is the subject of the sentence which has as its main verb *wins*. The noun clause is more fully integrated into the main clause than the adverbial clause would be:

If someone is daring, he will win.

Also, being defined entirely by its function in the complex sentence, a noun clause has no predictable range of subordinating conjunctions. You would expect *if the work is finished* to be an adverb clause of possibility, but look at the following sentence:

I don't know if the work is finished.

The clause is the direct object of *don't know* and, thus, a noun clause.

Adjective clauses

The integration of an adjective clause (or adnominal relative clause) into a complex sentence is again different from either adverb or noun clauses. This modifies a noun and therefore it can occupy two different places in the sentence:
1 next to the noun/noun phrase it modifies;
2 after a verb of being as the intensive complement.

Misplaced adjectival clauses can cause confusion:

The Northern Manager decided to pay a call on the branch *which coincided with his visit to Northumberland*.

On the other hand, a lengthy adjectival clause mid-sentence can be ugly and equally confusing:

The Northern Manager decided to pay a call *which coincided with his visit to Northumberland* on the branch.

A little tinkering with word order can often bring results:

The Northern Manager decided to pay the branch a call *which coincided with his visit to Northumberland.*

Relating the subordinate clause

With its subject and finite verb the subordinate clause has a fair amount of freedom to act on its own: we cannot be confused about who did the act or when. However, the clause remains subordinate. The subordinating conjunction or relative pronoun means that it exists only in inferior relationship to something else: the main clause or another subordinate clause or some element like a noun within another clause.

You need to be absolutely clear what your subordinate clause relates to. Examine the following examples in which the subordinate clauses are italicized:

I decided to trust Kerrigan with the message *although he was rather forgetful* I thought at least he would be tactful.

The fireworks went off *when midnight struck* the crowd burst into shouts, cheers and the occasional song.

It was difficult to find our way on the mountain, scrambling down the rocky slopes *as darkness fell swiftly and no lights could be seen*, we found ourselves beneath a crag we had never seen before.

These are three examples of a common error. The subordinate clause in the middle could relate to the main clause either before it or after it. You must choose which one you want:

either

I decided to trust Kerrigan with the message although he was rather forgetful. I thought at least he would be tactful.

or

I decided to trust Kerrigan with the message. Although he was rather forgetful, I thought at least he would be tactful.

No connection has been made between the two main clauses by means of a co-ordinating conjunction or even a suitable punctuation mark (colon/semicolon). Therefore they remain separate sentences, not the halves of a compound sentence. The third example has been deliberately chosen as a longer sentence with more clauses because this sort of situation makes the error more likely. However, the difficulty coming down the mountain and the sight of the crag are not joined syntactically, no matter how much you write about the coming of darkness.

Compound-complex sentences

For ease of analysis we have been treating compound and complex sentences as though they are completely different from each other. This is necessary to establish the connections between different elements in a sentence, but it oversimplifies sentence structure. Read the following sentence and decide how it has been put together:

> When the January sales start, the larger stores experience huge crowds and usually stay open late so that they can satisfy the demand.

At the centre of the sentence are two **co-ordinate main clauses** (with the verbs *experience* and *stay*). The first of these main clauses has a subordinate adverbial clause of time (*When the January sales start*) attached to it; the second main clause leads on to an adverbial clause of purpose (*so that they can satisfy the demand*). So what is this perfectly normal sentence to be called? Predictably it is known as a **compound-complex sentence.**

Compound-complex sentences combine all the characteristics of both forms of sentence. A co-ordinating conjunction or a suitable punctuation mark joins the main clauses and each main clause accumulates subordinate clauses on the basis described earlier in the chapter. As with any complex sentence, the writer needs to be clear about exactly what any subordinate clause relates to. Two further examples (the second using a colon rather than a conjunction) may clarify further:

Examples of compound-complex sentences:
  A If we can get a cheap fare to Malaga (1), I would like to go for Christmas (2), but, if it means paying too much (3), I would be

quite happy to stay here (4) and visit the relations (5) when our Welsh cousins come over on Boxing Day (6).

B The group has decided to put on *Bedroom Farce* (1): it is a very popular play (2) which will build on the good audiences (3) we got (4) when we last did an Ayckbourn (5).

Sentence A has three co-ordinate main clauses (2, 4 and 5) joined by co-ordinating conjunctions: I *would like to go for Christmas, but* ... I *would be quite happy to stay here and visit the relations*. Each of these has an adverbial clause attached to it: 1 and 3 of possibility (using *if*), 6 of time (using *when*).

Sentence B is a quite different structure: the two co-ordinate main clauses (1 and 2) begin the sentence separated by a colon as 2 is an explanation of 1. Clause 2 then sets up a family tree of subordinate clauses: two relative adjective/adnominal clauses: 3 modifying *play* in the co-ordinate main clause 2, then 4 modifying *audiences* in subordinate clause 3. The omission of relative pronoun *which* in front of *we got* is common. Finally an adverbial clause of time (5) modifies clause 4.

The analysis of these sentences makes them sound complicated, but they do not seem such on reading or hearing. The reason for this is that, while hardly elegant English, they are examples of correctly interlocking clauses relating exactly to each other.

It is worth emphasizing at this point that subordinate clauses can attract the same range of additional clauses as a main clause. Let us take the sentence:

The wind blew fiercely *and* the thunder crashed.

That is an orthodox compound sentence, but we can very easily add the subordinating conjunction *when* to the start of the sentence and add a new main clause:

When the wind blew fiercely and the thunder crashed,
    we quickly took shelter.

The first part of the sentence becomes what we might term a compound subordinate clause.

Parentheses

All the above make the English language sound precisely structured. Those who read, write and (especially) speak or listen to it know this not to be the case. Informal speech, of course, need not abide by the rules of sentence construction, though many a formal speech maker plants his or her pauses carefully to place subordinate clauses with the correct statements.

Even in formal written English it is possible to include inserts which have no grammatical connection to the surrounding sentence. Such inserts are known as **parentheses** and can be marked by brackets, dashes or commas. It is important to include the punctuation mark at each end of the parenthesis unless it runs up to the end of the sentence and a terminal point (full stop, etc.). Take the following example:

> With the appearance of Inspector Bucket – Dickens was, incidentally, the first major English novelist to feature a detective and his methods – the sins and sufferings of the Dedlock family are woven into the main stream of human crime and misery.

The point being made about Dickens and the detective is a suitable case for parenthesis as its connection with the main point of the sentence is oblique, not direct. In the following sentence a straightforward relative clause is more suitable:

> With the character of Inspector Bucket, whose mixture of underground contacts, tenacity and eccentricity must have been striking to the original readers, Dickens paves the way for the many sleuths and investigators who followed later in the 19th century.

However, the use of parenthesis is very much a matter of taste and over-indulgence can seem mannered as well as spreading confusion among readers.

punctuation

If we are to communicate clearly in English, we need to be able to spell accurately, but spelling is not an essential part of grammar, simply a code that conveys the meaning of words. This is less true of punctuation which is an essential aid to syntax in revealing the form and nature of sentences.

There are elements in punctuation where personal preference can prevail – a preference for dashes over brackets, for instance, or an enthusiasm or distaste for semi-colons – but these are comparatively rare. A correct use of terminal punctuation is vital unless a creative writer rejects it in the interests of art. Colons and semi-colons need to be distinguished from each other, the details of speech punctuation and of the various functions of the apostrophe need to be mastered and (most common fault of all) the excessive use of the comma needs to be restrained.

Terminal points

Each sentence ends with a terminal point, followed by a capital letter at the beginning of the next sentence. It is hardly necessary to point out the differences between **full stop, question mark** and **exclamation mark**, but you might like to note:

* A **question mark** is used when the form of the sentence is a question, not when the speaker is expecting an answer. *I wonder if you can tell me the time.* is followed by a full stop although an answer is expected whereas *Would you mind being quiet?* keeps its question mark although it is an implied command, answerable by silence.

* Most of the full sentences ending in **exclamation marks** do so by the choice of the writer: the tone of voice or the style of the article determines whether *Now we are going to swim with the dolphins* ends with full stop or exclamation mark.

Colons (:) and semicolons (;)

The semicolon

It is probably as well to see a semicolon as occupying the territory between a full stop and a comma. In other words, if a full stop seems too terminal or a comma too temporary a pause, there is a role for the semicolon. Two main clauses may not be linked by any conjunction, yet seem too close in meaning to be separate sentences:

In the morning the Geography paper was really hard; the English in the afternoon was much better.

It is, of course, a matter of choice: a full stop would also be correct and there is scope for a subordinate clause, perhaps using *whereas*.

The other use is when a comma seems inadequate. A list is punctuated by commas, but what if each item in the list is lengthy, with various commas in use?

We took with us to the party a bottle of white wine, though we failed to find their favourite Chablis; all the presents, including those Jane had sent from Scotland; a couple of CDs we thought would interest them; the birthday cake we had promised and a special bottle opener to add to Steve's collection of gadgets.

You could punctuate that solely with commas, but it would be very difficult to follow. With such long and clumsy phrases, some writers would even favour inserting another semicolon after '...we had promised'.

The colon

The **colon** has two specific purposes. Placed in the middle of a sentence, it introduces a section that explains, amplifies or completes what has gone before: this may be in terms of a reasoned account (as in this present sentence) or simply a list. As so often, the function of a colon is best illustrated by examples:

Rovers were playing with a back four: Bell, Miller, Jones and Doyle. (first half amplified by list)

Seville Cathedral is a dominating structure: it is said to be bigger than St Paul's. (first half amplified by clause adding extra facts)

Eric was worried about his health: a check-up proved negative. (first half completed by clause)

I decided not to go to Australia after all: the prospect of such a long flight put me off. (first half explained by clause)

If you use the colon in this way, do not insert a subordinating conjunction. The alternative to the last example would be:

I decided not to go to Australia after all because the prospect of such a long flight put me off.

The second purpose of a colon could be defined as introducing speech, although that is not quite accurate. For ordinary speech, though a colon is acceptable, a comma is preferable. However, colons are rightly used for examples or extended quotations, perhaps from a newspaper or a work of literature, as in the following example:

> Hamlet at this stage appears to be contemplating suicide:
> 'To be or not to be, that is the question...'

The addition of a dash to the colon is not encouraged.

Dashes and hyphens

Unfortunately these can appear identical (correctly the dash is longer than the hyphen) although they have very different, almost opposite functions. A *dash* is essentially a piece of sentence punctuation, dividing parts of a sentence, whereas a *hyphen* usually links single words.

Dashes

A major function of the dash (or, usually, of a pair of dashes) is to separate a **parenthesis** (or **parenthetical phrase**) from the rest of the sentence:

> Our itinerary includes a visit to Dubrovnik – the ancient walled city has now undergone successful restoration following the civil wars – before resuming the cruise through the Adriatic.

A parenthesis is an insert which does not form part of the grammatical structure of the sentence. Sometimes a phrase which could be absorbed syntactically is treated as a parenthesis because it seems like an insert or afterthought:

> The problem with dashes – and also with brackets – is knowing when to use them.

A parenthesis can also be indicated with **brackets** (properly, but confusingly, known as parentheses). This is a matter of preference, but consistency helps to improve your English style: perhaps brackets for short phrases, dashes for clauses or non-finite clauses. Remember that, once opened, brackets must be closed;

dashes must also be repeated, unless the end of the sentence intervenes.

Dashes also have a useful function as the most informal of punctuation marks: to indicate a gap or interruption, to hold the tension for a pause before a comic or dramatic resolution:

> 'I need to see you to talk about –' Suddenly the line went dead. The main speaker slowly stepped forward, surveyed the audience with a patronizing smile, placed his speech on the lectern – and knocked the water jug all over the first page.

Hyphens

The main function of hyphens is to join two words or sometimes prefix and stem, to form a word that may exist as a dictionary entry or may be created for the occasion. For instance, *anti-personnel* (meaning 'intending to harm people') exists as a word; movements to outlaw pugilism or beauty contests would be termed *anti-boxing* or *anti-Miss World*.

This fusion of words via hyphens can take various forms, including, of course, names (*Anne-Marie* or *Lloyd-Roberts*) and set phrases, often of more than two words (*out-of-date*, *happy-go-lucky*). A pair of words might make a progress over the years from being two separate words to being hyphenated to being one word and it is often difficult to be sure where along that journey any word is. Inconsistencies abound: we are *hardbitten*, but *hard-hearted* and *hard up*. Hyphens are often used when an noun or adjective phrase is used before the noun: we use *common sense*, but take a *common-sense attitude*.

Apostrophes and quotation marks / inverted commas

Some guides to English write that single quotation marks are used for the main speech and double for a quotation, inside the speech. A preference for double quotation marks is, however, generally acceptable, but it is important to reverse the form for a secondary quotation:

> The new trainee said, 'I'm sorry I missed what you said. Did you say, "Turn right at the double doors"?'

or The new trainee said, "I'm sorry I missed what you said. Did you say, 'Turn right at the double doors'?"

The example above illustrates the important rule about punctuation marks (most noticeably exclamation and question marks) in speech. If the question/exclamation is within the speech, the punctuation mark is inside the quotation marks. In the example the trainee is asking a question, but the other speaker did not ask a question: hence the placing of the question mark.

Remember that quotation marks surround **only the words actually spoken**. For *she said* or *he remarked*, the quotation marks close and re-open:

> 'I remember that holiday in Greece,' she said, 'where we all suffered with sunburn.'

Quotation marks can be used to suggest that the word you are using may not be true (the equivalent of 'so-called') or is a title not yet proven. Generally nowadays titles of books, films, albums, etc., are indicated by italics, but quotation marks are common for the titles of chapters, articles, songs, etc. So you would refer to the song 'With a little help from my friends' from the Beatles' album *Sergeant Pepper's Lonely Hearts Club Band*.

Apostrophes

The basic purpose of apostrophes is to indicate the omission of letters in the middle of a word: *we'll*, *didn't*, *Hallowe'en*, *it's* (only when it means *it is* or *it has*).

Occasionally an apostrophe will be used for an omitted letter at the beginning of a word ('*cello* for *violoncello*), but this is not necessary. Omissions at the end of a word are indicated by a full stop: *Co.* for *Company*. Also such abbreviations as *Mr.* and *Mrs.*

(for *Mister* and, originally, *Mistress*) traditionally employ a full stop when an apostrophe might seem more logical. The current tendency to economize on punctuation in titles and addresses means that it is now common to omit the full stops, certainly in print (as in this book).

It is widely thought that the other use of apostrophes (to indicate **possession**) stems from a misunderstanding of the omission rule. Formerly possession was simply indicated by an *s*, but the belief that this was short for *his* led to the inclusion of the apostrophe. When indicating singular possession, '*s* follows the noun. Plurals in *s* form possession by adding the apostrophe after the *s*:

> The missing girl's school has not been disclosed.
> Most schools are mixed, but there is a girls' school in the town.
> The bank's policy is not to give unsecured loans.
> The banks' merger should strengthen their financial base.

The comma

Left until the end, the comma is the punctuation mark with either the least or the most functions of all. If you attempt to define the different functions of a comma, the list seems almost endless: adjectives or nouns in a list, introducing speech, dividing many forms of subordinate clause from the main clause or each other, following written salutations, etc. On the other hand the role of the comma can be defined as making a necessary short pause or division between elements that are nonetheless closely linked. A comma asks the reader to distinguish between the elements on each side of it, but not to make a fresh start.

The main weakness in use of the comma is, in fact, overuse, especially where a full stop, semicolon or colon is needed. Though a pair of commas can mark a parenthesis, this is advisable only in short parentheses; otherwise sentence structure disappears beneath the various different applications of commas. The two following sentences are good examples of the use of the comma for a parenthesis:

> The car, incidentally, has had to go in for service.
> The path by the beach, the 'prom' as we called it, was under several inches of water.

but not:

> When it became obvious that the fire was out, the chief officer, with a wry smile, his good temper had been undisturbed throughout, congratulated us on our good luck.

The parenthesis, 'his good temper...throughout', needs dashes or brackets.